George Linnaeus Banks

Forbidden to marry

Vol. I

George Linnaeus Banks

Forbidden to marry
Vol. I

ISBN/EAN: 9783337040116

Printed in Europe, USA, Canada, Australia, Japan

Cover: Foto ©ninafisch / pixelio.de

More available books at **www.hansebooks.com**

FORBIDDEN TO MARRY.

BY

MRS. G. LINNÆUS BANKS,

AUTHORESS OF "GOD'S PROVIDENCE HOUSE;" "THE MANCHESTER
MAN;" "GLORY," &c., &c.

A Novel.

IN THREE VOLUMES.

VOL. I.

LONDON:
F. V. WHITE & CO., 31, SOUTHAMPTON ST., STRAND.
1883.

CONTENTS.

CHAPTER	PAGE
I.—Preliminary	1
II.—Settled	19
III.—Travellers	32
IV.—At the Forest House	55
V.—Red Riding-Hood and Her Friends	79
VI.—Left with the Misses Briscoe	102
VII.—Muriel's New Life	118
VIII.—Mrs. Hopley's Postscript	140
IX.—A Proposal	163
X.—Sam's First	185
XI.—Muriel's Return Home	203

FORBIDDEN TO MARRY.

CHAPTER I.

PRELIMINARY.

"WHAT! nursing again, Muriel! What is Betty doing, and where is thy mother?" cried Mrs. Bancroft, the furrier, as she walked into the back parlour of her son-in-law's house, the mere turn of a handle having opened the front entrance for her, without the ceremony of knocking. It was only when rioters or other rough people were about that doors were bolted during daylight in the last century, or indeed in the early years of this. A slim girl, not more than eleven years of age, was pacing the floor with a baby-brother in her slender arms. She answered cheerfully;

"Betty is washing dishes in the back kitchen, and mother is upstairs putting the clean clothes away. I have not had Georgey very long, grandmother. And I don't mind nursing him one bit when he doesn't cry. He has given over now."

"Oh! then he has been crying?" and there was some acerbity in the old lady's tone, as if *she* had "minded" very much.

"A little. Poor fellow, his teeth plague him, mother says;" and Muriel D'Anyer bent over the big boy in her arms with such a look of pitiful affection in her large dark-brown eyes, as clearly told she was in earnest, though he did make her arms ache, and her heart too when she could not still his complaining.

"I suppose Anna and Marion are both at school?" again questioned Mrs. Bancroft. "And where is Sara?"

"Upstairs with mother. Hsh, hsh,"—this to the infant, whose lip was again curling to a cry.

The old lady's chintz gown of printed linen was open in the front over a quilted petticoat, though tucked up behind to keep her train out of the dust, and on each side, under this open robe, a pannier-like pocket balanced its fellow. By a bright steel chain depended from her waist the sheathed scissors and plump pincushion, without which no good housewife was equipped. Her keys would have dangled from another chain, but that out of doors they were slipped into the right-hand pocket, and were consequently invisible, even the chain being lost under the over-gown. It was summer-time, and a scarf-like mantle of black silk covered her shoulders, as mittens covered her arms, leaving her fingers bare and free to use; the bonnet on her head towered high above her lappet-like cap, and assisted by her high-heeled shoes (buckled across the instep) imparted height and importance to a short figure.

Emptying from one pocket a store of cherries, and cakes from the other, she kissed the girl on the forehead, and said, "Divide these amongst you," and without waiting for thanks quitted the room and marched upstairs.

She found her daughter, Mrs. D'Anyer—quite a young-looking woman to be the mother of five children—on her knees in front of a carved oaken coffer, her own gift to the married couple. She was counting and arranging her household sheets and napery fresh from the airing, with little Sara, a fair-haired beauty of three years, watching her movements, and hindering under the pretext of help.

Without a word of prelude Mrs. Bancroft began, in a broader vernacular than I care to inflict on my readers, common as it was then to the manufacturing class;

"I tell thee what, Ellen, I shall not leave Muriel here any longer to be kept from school, and sacrificed to that boy. She is not strong enough."

Mrs. D'Anyer rose to salute her mother, but her gentle "How do you do?" changed to a faltering apology, "Well, mother, I should not have kept her at home to-day, but I was very busy——"

"And always will be" interrupted her

mother: "every day brings its own duties, and every household its own work; only contrivance and management can keep the hour's work to the hour. But busy or not busy, I'm not going to see Muriel grow lopsided with lugging a great lad about, and grow up in ignorance whilst her sisters are being properly educated. Thah must have a nurse if Betty has no time. I know thah't not so strong as thah should be—all the fruits of marrying too young—and thah needs help; but I don't think John will mind thee keeping a stout lass to nurse that lad of his. If he does, *I'll* pay her wages; and as I mean to take Muriel off your hands altogether, that will square accounts."

Mrs. D'Anyer, a mild, timid little woman, stood in no small awe of her prompt, energetic mother, but she also stood in fear of her husband, and ventured a sort of expostulatory protest, to which the old lady paid no sort of heed.

"I tell thee, Ellen," she maintained, "the eldest girl in a large family is always made a drudge to the rest; it was so in my case, but I'll take care it shall not be Muriel's lot. She shall go home with me; I'll see her educated. John won't miss her. I don't think he has cared for the lass since the illness that seamed her face and spoiled her beauty;" and she wiped a handkerchief over her own face, warm with the excitement and energy of her speech.

"Oh, mother!" was all the younger woman could interject in remonstrance, as she placed the last pile of linen in the coffer and closed the heavy lid.

"Ah, thah may say, 'Oh, mother!' but thah knows its true. I'll go and have a talk to John in the warehouse. I suppose I shall find him there;" and off she went, determined not to let her project cool.

It has been said that Mrs. Bancroft was a furrier. It may be added that she had for many years carried on most successfully the extensive wholesale business of her dead husband, in premises situated in the rear of her handsome double-fronted red brick house on Red Bank, Manchester, and was accounted a wealthy woman in her sphere. Wealthy, that is, as the world goes; her possessions could be reckoned in houses and land, bought and sold as merchandise; but she had scarcely the true riches, though she went regularly to church, stood in good repute, and had a profound veneration for religious profession in others.

Dingy enough now is the thoroughfare known as Red Bank; even fifty years ago the deterioration had begun, smoke doing more than the finger of Time to tone down tints of brickwork and stone; nay, a publican had set his sign over what had been Mrs. Bancroft's door, there were shops where had been private houses, and inferior structures were creeping up the steep hill-sides to obliterate every trace of grass or of the red sand from which the road took its name. Yet was the verdant country close at hand in Mrs. Bancroft's time, grass and flowers and bushes were plentiful atop of the rugged redbanks left on either side by successive lowerings of the hill, over which then ran the main road to Rochdale and Bury from Scotland Bridge and the valley of the Irk upwards, and Mrs. Bancroft's house at the foot of the brow was a residence of some pretensions.

Twelve years prior to this decided enunciation of opinion relative to her favourite grandchild Muriel, her own daughter Ellen was a dark-haired, dark-eyed, vivacious damsel of sixteen, the youthful roundness of whose cheeks softened the high cheek-bones, which age or illness might define and sharpen as they had done for the elder woman. They were alike short in stature, alike active and notable, but the resolute set of mouth and the energy of the woman had no signs of development in the girl.

At that period dancing was an accomplishment more for the aristocracy than for traders, but a certain Madam Bland had opened an academy in a fashionable part of the town for such as could afford to pay well for instruction, and Mrs. Bancroft did not hesitate to enrol Ellen among the select circle of Madam

Bland's pupils, as a finishing touch to an education which had, to say the least, cost much.

No retail trader could have gained admission for son or daughter into that circle; the line was drawn at merchants and manufacturers; but of all those who did most honour to Madam's professorship was John D'Anyer, who, though but the son of a Manchester manufacturer, yet boasted he had blue blood in his veins as in his name.

He was barely twenty, yet he stood six feet high, and had a figure as finely proportioned as his handsome face. Dancing was only one of his many accomplishments, but it was the one in which his peculiar graces of form and manner were most likely to move impressionable hearts; and Ellen Bancroft was only one of the damsels who sighed for him. But in her case the attraction was mutual. And not alone in minuet or cotillion had they seen and admired each other. The Bancroft and the D'Anyer pews in the Collegiate Church adjoined, there was speaking acquaintance between the elders, and the two young people might be said to have grown up under each other's eye.

In Madam Bland's academy the acquaintance ripened rapidly; it furnished occasions for mutual intercourse unsuspected at home, and led to a step not in the Terpsichorean programme.

One sunny morning when early May blossoms scented the air, Miss Bancroft, arrayed as for a fashionable assembly in a dress of cherry colour-and-white satin brocade, her hair elaborately coiled by the peruquier, was handed by her admiring mother into a sedan chair at the door of the house on Red Bank, as was customary on dancing days, and it slightly struck the mother that "the lass was in an unusual flurry."

Be this as it may, the chairmen bore the sedan, not to Madam Bland's, but to the Collegiate Church; and when they again set her down at her unsuspecting mother's door she was the wife of John D'Anyer.

No one's advice had been asked, no one's

counsel taken. The girl, captivated by a handsome face and graceful figure, had allowed his dominant will to control her. Had any reason existed for secrecy beyond their immature age, it was unknown.

Three months later a loud ran-tan, tan, tan, tan, on the heavy knocker, startled the echoes in the Red Bank house. Mrs. Bancroft had just come in from the warehouse for her four o'clock tea, and a maid was carrying the mahogany tea-board, with its freight of tiny handleless cups and saucers, into the household room, and almost dropped it in her fright.

The clang on the knocker had not ceased when she opened the door, and Mr. John D'Anyer, in a fashionable suit of plum-coloured kerseymere, with silver buckles at his breeches' knees and on the instep of his high-heeled shoes, crushed past her into the lobby, and in thick but imperious tones demanded to see his "wife."

Margery insisted that he had mistaken the house, and failing to convince him, turned back to seek her mistress in the kitchen.

To her amazement he followed her, not too steadily, down the passage, to be confronted by Mrs. Bancroft, who stood with her face towards him, by the white deal table, under the broad window, at which Ellen was washing, in a large bowl, lace ruffles and lawn kerchiefs, too dainty to be sent to a common clear-starcher.

It was evident the young man had taken too much wine; his three-cornered hat was awry, the ruffles at his wrists, the falling neckcloth edged with lace, were sullied and disordered; and so Mrs. Bancroft thought were his wits, as he repeated, "I have come for my wife; I want my wife."

"Your wife?" she echoed, and would have added, "There is no wife of yours here," but she chanced to glance towards her daughter, and the words died upon her lips.

It needed not his iteration of "Yes, Ellen;—my wife!" that white face, that shrinking, trembling figure told all.

Whether in wrath, or to keep the girl from fainting, she could never decide with herself, she took up the earthen bowl and dashed its contents, water and lace together, upon the daughter who had deceived her.

"Take your wife, take her! and never let her darken my doors again!" she cried, sternly, and passed out of the kitchen, not to return until the door had closed upon them both, as *she* had closed the door of her heart.

Though an only daughter, Ellen was not an only child. She had a brother three years her senior, training to succeed his mother in the business. His intercession for his sister might have been expected.

Nothing of the kind occurred. Samuel Bancroft had not a thought beyond self. He sat down to the tea-table, after a rough preliminary scrub in the scullery, rendered necessary by his duties in the skin-yard—was briefly told what had occurred, bidden never to name his sister again,—and had no desire to transgress.

He could have told, had he been so minded, that he had been deputed to break the secret

to his mother; but he preferred to assume
ignorance, and wipe his clean hands of the
offending pair, as he hoped to wipe his sister
out of the mother's will by-and-bye.

Months went by—months which sharpened
and hardened the outlines of Sarah Bancroft's
face. An idol had been shattered, and nothing
had replaced it. Her seat in the Old Church
was vacant; she resolutely passed its walls
and trudged forward to St. Ann's (there being
no church nearer home at that time); but
though she heard the words "Harden not
your hearts, as in the provocation," Sabbath
by Sabbath, she refused to take their import
to herself. If there was any softening of her
heart, it was unknown; the silence peremp-
torily enjoined at the outset became habitual;
her business did not throw her in the way
of the D'Anyers, and she knew nothing even
of her daughter's whereabouts. Whether she
felt more keenly the barb of her child's
ungrateful secrecy, or the prolonged estrange-
ment, could not be told; but unspoken feeling
of some kind brought out more sharply the

prominence of her cheek-bone, and ploughed fresh lines on her brow.

She had several brothers and brothers-in-law in different trades; but their places of business lying away across the town, they did not often meet.

One sleety afternoon in the following February, as she was shaking hands with a Bolton hatter, to whom she had sold a large parcel of rabbit-skins (to be felted into veritable beaver), her brother Ralph, a cotton merchant, stepped into the warehouse, amongst piles of skins, and barely waiting until the hatter's back was turned began,—

"Sarah, dost thah know the tale that's goin' about the town?"

"What tale?" said both eyes and lips.

"Why, that thy daughter Ellen was turned out of the house wringin' wet, with no clothes but what she stood up in, and is now livin' on the *charity* of the D'Anyers!"

Mrs. Bancroft changed countenance. "Wringing wet!" "No clothes!" she echoed, as if unaware how literally Ellen's dismissal had been taken, but her pride caught up the one word "charity," and her breast heaved as with a pent-up burden. "Charity! charity!" she exclaimed. "My daughter living upon *charity!* I'll see about that!" and to her brother's surprise, before he was aware of her intentions, she was across the yard, in the house, and out again at the front, with the hood of her scarlet cloth cloak over her bonnet, and her pattens on her feet, hurrying through the wet to the smallware manufacturer's in Cannon Street, panting as she went with suppressed and contending emotions.

"I hear that my daughter is said to be living on your *charity*, Mr. D'Anyer," she began abruptly, as the old smallware manufacturer presented himself before his unexpected visitor.

"Nay, nay, Mrs. Bancroft, Ellen is as welcome as th' flowers i' May. I put another loom down when she came, that's all, and I mean to put another down now th' little lass hath come! I always put a fresh loom down when a fresh mouth comes to be filled; and the more the merrier, say I. I only wish Nelly herself was stronger; but she has never fairly got over the wetting you gave her."

Mrs. Bancroft felt herself rebuked, though she did not take in the full purport of his speech. "Well, sir," said she, ignoring the censure, "you can put the profit of your looms to other uses. I do not intend *my* daughter to live an any one's *charity*. If your son has neither business to maintain his wife, nor home to take her to, it is time he had. And I'll tell you what I'll do. I'll furnish them a house, and I'll be five hundred pounds towards setting him up in business, if you'll be another five hundred; and they can come to *my* house until they have one of their own. But no living on *charity!*" and the word came out with a gasp.

"There has been no charity, my good friend," said Mr. D'Anyer, with a genial smile. "No one regretted John's secret and precipitate match more than myself and Mally" (his wife), "but my son's wife is my daughter, and as such we made her welcome. And I shall be glad to meet you half-way in giving them a start in life, either in my trade, or yours, or one of your brothers'. But they will have to stay here until they have a house of their own. We are not so thick on the spot as we were, and the place is big enough to hold us all. Besides—Ellen cannot be removed, and I don't think it would be safe for you to see her just yet; she must not be agitated. But there's naught to hinder you seeing the little lass."

"What little lass?" Mrs. Bancroft would have asked, but he was out of the room, and she who had gone there in high-handed pride and indignation, was left to institute comparisons and ponder his meaning. Presently he returned with a long-robed infant in his patriarchal arms—and then she was enlightened.

Pride, indignation, resentment, dissolved in tears over her first grandchild's face.

Little Muriel had come as a pacificator.

CHAPTER II.

SETTLED.

A THOUSAND pounds was a goodly capital to commence business with in 1778, when John D'Anyer elected to turn fustian manufacturer, a term at that time of very wide signification. A warehouse was found and fitted for his trade in Sugar Lane, not far from his own father's thread and smallware manufactory in Cannon Street. Then Mrs. Bancroft, reconciled to the young people, furnished for them, solidly and well, a house in Broom Street close by, the exclusive respectability of which was maintained by posts and chains to bar the ingress of unprivileged vehicles. Whatever the street may be now, it was then genteel—and dull; but Broom Street and Sugar Lane met at a sharp angle, and there was the advantage of communication at the back between house and warehouse. Steam power had not been introduced into manufactories, and very few were fitted up with elaborate machinery. Outlay was chiefly for raw material and work-people's wages. In John D'Anyer's, for instance, warpers—generally women—carried home great hanks of yarn in their canvas bags, or "pokes," and brought it back on their heads in huge flat balls, warped; that is, threads of sufficient number and length for the piece of cloth, arranged and grouped together systematically by means of pegs in the warper's cottage wall. The handloom weavers took home the warp, with twist for the weft, and brought it back in the piece; again it went out to be bleached or dyed, and, in the case of fustians, to be cut. In these days so many processes are carried on in one set of premises that immense capitals are required. Then John D'Anyer was considered to start under very favourable auspices, and expected to make a fortune, as others had done before him.

But they were plodders, he was not. He was proud to be his own master, and the master of others; had taken to the business kindly, and was not too proud to doff his coat and lend a hand either to putter-out or packer. Then, being vain of his penmanship, he conducted his own correspondence, not a very onerous duty, and kept his own books, with a clerk under him; and was as good a buyer and seller as any on 'Change. But he was vain of his person as well as of his penmanship, and was apt to vary the monotony of the Exchange Room with a stroll under the trees of St. Ann's Square, the adjacent fashionable promenade, or arm in arm with friend or cousin of his own age, who had more money than wit, finish the day at the cockpit, or it might be in a carouse.

And in this John D'Anyer must not be judged by our standard. Temperance had not become a creed: a man amongst men was he who could carry most liquor with the steadiest legs and the clearest head; and so long as a man was up and about his business during the day, no one troubled himself how he spent his nights. That concerned no one but the people at home.

And it must not be supposed that John D'Anyer's proclivity for convivial society was such as to interfere with his business, or make him other than a gentleman, although he had demanded his girl-wife in most unseemly fashion. He was wont to say he "would not give a button for any man who could not be anything in any society," and certainly the polished gentleman occasionally descended. He was, however, a strict disciplinarian in business or out, and his devoted little wife, who had not her mother's strength of will, was too timid to oppose act or word of his, too nervous to propose aught to which he might object; and neither years nor motherhood brought her self-reliance.

Mrs. Bancroft was loth to admit it even to herself; but Ellen D'Anyer had never quite recovered from the effects of the wetting she had given her twelve years before. Her imprudent and impetuous young husband, too

excited to reason, had hurried her away at
Mrs. Bancroft's harsh bidding, drenched as
she was; and though he hailed the first sedan
chair they met, there was nearly a mile to
traverse between Red Bank and Cannon
Street, and explanations to follow, before dry
garments could be substituted. Rheumatic
fever was a natural sequence, and life-long
delicacy; mental suffering having been super-
added to the physical. Her long illness had,
however, been borne with patient resignation,
and had served to draw her nearer to her
Creator. The seventeen-years-old wife had laid
down her self-will before Muriel was born.

It was therefore with no slight trepidation
she awaited, with her boy in her arms, the
return of her energetic parent from the warehouse that summer afternoon; having no
clear idea of the proposal to be made, or of
her husband's mood to receive it. Nor was
she much more assured by the triumphant
smile on Mrs. Bancroft's face as she walked
into the back sitting-room and bade Muriel
" take Sara and her doll into the kitchen."

"Well, it is settled," she began; "I am to find you a respectable and capable nursemaid, and Muriel is to be turned over to me."

"You are not going to take Muriel from me," put in Mrs. John D'Anyer faintly.

"Yes, I am; so have her box packed by this day week. I'll see you have a nurse before then; and, by-the-bye, put nothing in that is half worn. I'll see she has a fresh rig out before she goes."

"Goes where?" asked the wondering young mother.

"Why, to Chester, with me. Did I not tell you I was going to send her to school?"

Mrs. John D'Anyer's heart sank. She dearly loved her first-born, if the father did not; and the announcement was like a sentence of banishment to her.

"Chester! Oh, mother, surely there are good schools in Manchester; you would not send the dear girl so far away. And such a dangerous road--that terrible forest to cross. How could she ever come home for her holidays!"

"She will have no holidays.—You need not look so blank. I will see to the lass. And I'll get thy father's kinsman, the Rev. Thomas Bancroft, to look after her, so she'll be well off, for he's a good man. She would only be put upon at home; be at every one's beck and call; be nursemaid and scapegoat for the whole lot, and I've set my mind on making a clever woman of her. Aye, and a happy one into the bargain. She is going amongst ladies, to be treated like a lady. I'll see to that."

Tears sprang to the mother's eyes.

"Now, don't be silly," cried the observant grandmother; "the child's not gone yet, and won't go till Chester Fair; so there's all the time between this and Michaelmas to reconcile yourself, if you are so foolish as to need reconciling to a change which is for her good."

"But what of Muriel? it will break her tender heart!"

"Leave her to me, there shall be no breaking of hearts. I'll see to that. There might be some breaking of back if she stayed here much longer. And now call her in, and let us have tea. John will be in directly."

During this colloquy Marion and Anna, the one nine and the other seven, had come skipping home from school; but, kept in check by Muriel with grandmother's cherries and cakes, had remained discreetly in the large bright kitchen. And as children were seldom permitted to take tea with their elders, there was no hardship in sitting down at the round oak table to their brown bread and cans of milk, whilst father, mother, and grandmother drank tea and ate white bread and butter in the parlour; and unknown to them, two strong minds strove to convince a weak but warm-hearted mother that it was well the daughter she loved should be taken from her.

The hardship came to the children a week afterwards, when Sister Muriel went to stay with Grandmother Bancroft, and a stout girl of fifteen, rough and ready in her handling of them, was the only substitute. They had no forecast of the longer parting in store, yet they cried themselves to sleep.

Nor had Muriel when she was sent every morning up Red Bank for a draught of new milk at the farm-house by the stocks, "to bring a colour into her cheeks," as her grandmother said; or even when she was measured for new frocks, and shoes and bonnets and caps, and was provided with a fur muff and tippet of grey squirrel, and was told that she was going with Grandmother Bancroft to Chester Fair.

Chester Fair! Did not her father and uncles talk of it, and the business down there, for weeks before and after; and had she not seen the preparations made for her father's departure, the packing of his saddle-bags, the loading of his pistols! Surely it was a great event to her, a something to look forward to with glee. Muriel had no prescience and no fears. But the tender mother had; and though she had been enjoined to say nothing, and to let the child go away quietly; and though she knew that Muriel was dearer to "Grandmother Bancroft" than all her possessions, and that the resolute old lady was actuated by a sincere desire to promote the child's welfare, she could not let her go under a false impression, to waken to reality among strangers, and that without a word of farewell warning and counsel.

She took the opportunity when Muriel, taller, stronger, and rosier for her four months' residence and rambles in the fresh air and green fields around Red Bank—the latter shared with Milly Hargreaves, a favourite cousin, whose father's dye-works lay between Red Bank and the River Irk—was permitted to spend a couple of days in Broom Street prior to the eagerly anticipated journey to Chester Fair.

Never to be forgotten by Muriel so long as she lived, was that hour with her mother in the privacy of her chamber, an hour dark as was the mahogany furniture and heavy moreen draperies, for there she first learned that her journey to Chester was not a mere pleasure-trip. It was sad for both; not that the Misses Briscoe's school had terrors for Muriel, or to Mrs. John D'Anyer; it had been painted in the brightest tints; but the parting, the separation for a long and uncertain period, the distance which must lie between them, had. And to understand this, it must be known that in 1789 there was no direct conveyance for passengers between Manchester and Chester. Goods were sent on pack-horses, or by the Duke of Bridgewater's new canal; and horse-drawn packet-boats which met a stage-coach three miles from Frodsham, were also provided for the accommodation of passengers. Otherwise the ordinary stage-coach went no farther than Northwich, and people who did not travel on horse-back must hire a post-chaise or a cart, and run the risk of highwaymen and footpads on their route through Delamere Forest, if they wished to reach the Palatine city.

These dangers had been too often discussed in Muriel's presence to leave her ignorant. There could be no home-coming at stated times, and her young heart sank; but when she saw how her dearly-loved mother was overpowered, she put a brave face upon it, and said " perhaps father or grandmother might bring her mother over to see her at fair time." She knew that her grandmother had a relation in Chester, a clergyman, the head master of the Grammar School there, and had been told that he would be sure to come and see her; still, he was not her mother, and her mother was all the world to her.

But she grew grave and sober as her mother exhorted her to " hold fast by the hand of Christ at all times and in all seasons, whether tried, or tempted, or troubled, and never to let it go." And then her mother put into her hands a thickly bound black volume with massive silver clasps, on which were engraved D.M., 1711, the same initials and date being stamped in gold on either side. " Take this, my child," she said; " it is the most precious token of my love that I can bestow upon you—the Bible and Prayer-book of our ancestress Deborah Massey; it was her constant companion, the law of her life. Make it yours, Muriel, and I shall never regret this day. The book has been handed down as a precious treasure; it has been such to me, let it be such to you."

The tears of the mother and daughter mingled on the black cover and on the silver clasps, as the arms of Muriel went round that mother's neck in a clasp as close, and a kiss of assurance sealed the promise that she gave.

CHAPTER III.

TRAVELLERS.

DELAMERE FOREST and Chester Fair! There was a promise of romance and mystery in the one, of pleasure in the other. What girl of Muriel's age but would have looked forward with excitement and anticipation?

It was a sad damper to learn that the romance of the hazardous journey, the show and delights of the great fair, were to terminate in the reality of a strange boarding-school, and long absence from home and the mother she loved so dearly.

Gratitude to Grandmother Bancroft, which had been bubbling up from the deep fountain in her breast, as one new garment after another had come from the mantuamaker, and her handsome furs from the warehouse, sank to a low ebb when she learned the hidden motive for so much preparation. It was not in her nature to demur openly, but she said to herself over and over again: " But for mother, I might have gone away without knowing! It was not kind of Grandmother Bancroft! It was *not kind*. How *could* she do it?" Her murmurings were, however, stilled by the remembrance that her own mother had said "it was for her good, and that it was very kind of grandmother to take the charge and expense of Muriel's wardrobe and education on herself." "If mother thinks it is good for me, I suppose I *ought* to be satisfied; and if grandmother really means it for the best, it is ungrateful to grumble. Only it is *so* far! Well, as mother says, the Lord can hear me, and see me, and care for me in Chester as well as here, and for them too!" but she had her fears, misgivings, and regrets, nevertheless.

It was in such mood Muriel watched her Grandmother Bancroft as she packed new linen and new frocks in a small trunk, covered

with mottled cow-hide, whereon her initials
" M. D." shone in the glory of brass nails.

"Who gave thee this?" asked Mrs. Bancroft, as the girl tendered the silver-clasped Bible to be packed.

"Mother," was the answer, "and see the letters on the back are the same as those on the box."

"I think Ellen might have set more store by Deborah Massey's Bible than to give it thee. But see thah take care of it, and use it well."

She did not say, "Make good use of it," *that* did not occur to her.

"But how is my box to go, grandmother?" asked Muriel, as the key was turned in the lock, and a canvas cover fitted; "if I am to ride on a pillion behind Uncle Sam, our horse could not carry it, and yours will have the saddle-bags. Will one of the pack-horses take it?"

"No, lass! I've done with pack-horses, thank goodness! Your box will go to-morrow along with the bales of furs and peltry to the wharfinger of the Duke's canal, and be sent by boat to Frodsham, or nigh it, and on by carrier's waggon to the Manchester Hall in Chester; the new hall that thy Grandfather D'Anyer, and me, and your uncles, and other Manchester folk have gone shares to build."

So saying, Mrs. Bancroft sent the packing-needle on its last errand through the canvas, drew the stitch tight with a business-like jerk, cut it away with the scissors at her girdle, and rose from her knees.

Muriel was curious.

"How did you manage, grandmother, before the hall was built?"

"How? Why, as best we could. Showed our goods in booths in the streets, as had been done for years before, or kept them at our inns, and looked out for customers. But that didn't suit me. I said I'd see about it, and now we've a fine hall to cover us."

"Hundreds of years!" Muriel had ejaculated, but Mrs. Bancroft's task completed, she had no mind to linger. She was wanted in the warehouse, else she might have told

Muriel that fairs were of very ancient date, and had their origin in the wants and necessities of the people; and that of the early English fairs, established and chartered for the sale or interchange of goods and produce, or for the hiring of men and maidservants at a period when towns and villages were scattered and far apart, roads few and unsafe, Chester Fair was one of the earliest, and in best repute. Its charter dated back almost to the days of Hugh Lupus, the first Earl of Chester, who held his rich Palatinate by grant from his near kinsman, William the Conqueror. Chester was an important seaport then, and needed a strong hand to fortify the castle the Romans had left, as well as to protect the commerce of the Dee from the pirates swarming in the Irish Channel. She might have told how the monks of St. Werburgh had represented " mysteries " or " miracle plays," to edify and keep from mischief the idle multitudes who thronged to the fair for sport, of which the more modern show was the outcome; and how none but freemen of the city were permitted to trade within its walls except when a white glove was hung out from the tower of St. Peter's, as a symbol of peace, of the native trade, and of the fair. And she might have justified her own special business at Chester Fair with an old chronicler's summary of its merchandise :—

> "Hides and fish, salmon, hake, herringe,
> Irish wool and linen cloth, faldinge,
> And martens good, be her marchandie,
> Hartes hides, and other of venerie,
> Skins of otter, squirrel, and Irish hose,
> Of sheep, lamb, and foxe, is her chaffare,
> Fells of kids and conies great plenty."

But she could not have told or foretold how "kettles o' steeam" would go whizzing and fizzing over the land with a besom of progression in their train to sweep such chartered fairs clean away as nuisances, not conveniences.

She had told the girl at various times quite sufficient about Chester, its fairs, and its double rows of shops, where the covered pathway to the upper row was right over the roofs of the lower set, above which the prominent house-fronts formed a sort of arcade; quite enough to put the looming school in the background, and after the first tears of parting were dried, to cause Muriel to sit her pillion lightly, and clasp her Uncle Sam's waist in hopeful mood and with a smile on her cheerful countenance.

But Muriel had never mounted a pillion before; the journey was long and tedious; the roads were wofully uneven beneath the horse's feet, and long ere they reached Northwich she was sick with the jolting, and her face proclaimed it. Samuel grumbled hard at the loss of time and money, when his mother announced her intention to remain at the Unicorn until the next morning on the lass's account.

"It's not as if you were going right through to Chester," he urged; "it's only seven or eight miles to Eddisbury, and you know the Kingsleys expect you. When Muriel has had a good dinner and a horn of home-brewed, she'll be as right as ninepence, I'll warrant."

It was not customary in the last century to discuss business before young people, or make them privy to the plans of their elders, and Muriel took the sharp "Sam!" and the significant frown of her grandmother, as a reminder that she was present, and need not be enlightened; but Samuel, keen and sharp where his own interest was concerned, took it as a hint that there were strangers in the room, and that it was not wise to prate of their path so openly.

Irritated as much at his own thoughtlessness as at the rebuke, he rubbed his hands smartly over his breeches' thighs, indulged in a brief whistle, and rising, said:

"Hang it, what a while they are with that dinner! I'll go and have a look at the horses, and see no tricks are played with them or their feed. One need be sharp in this world!" and the cunning look in his greenish-grey eyes said people had need to be very sharp indeed to take *him* in. At the door he turned round to say, "And if the lass be so desperately tired let her lie down on yon settle by the wall, if its cushion's soft enough," a hint Muriel scarcely liked to take before strangers.

But her grandmother's quick, "I'll see to that," settled the business, and she lay down, with a saddle-bag for a pillow, glad to rest, and in the sense of repose soon forgot the strangeness of all around, the farmers and others by the fire. Then she began to wonder if she also was expected at Eddisbury, and what sort of people the Kingsleys were, and what sort of a place the Forest House was, and to think how funny it was she should be going there after all her wonder about it. She had heard it spoken of many a time, but curiosity was a crime in that generation (and the next). "Don't ask questions, children should be seen and not heard," being the general stopper on a thirst for knowledge.

She had a hazy recollection of being told by some one it was "only an old, rambling farmhouse," and very likely her informant had no acquaintance with its history, and could have told her no more. But that old, rambling, picturesque, black-and-white, timber-and-rubble Forest House, of which scarcely a vestige remains for the antiquary, occupied the site of an older edifice still, the stronghold of the wise Ethelfleda, the daughter of King Alfred, the wife and widow of Ethelred, king of Mercia, the sister and counsellor of King Edward. Here, on a lofty elevation, in the very centre of the great forest, she, whom the old chroniclers call "the wisest of women," founded what she held to be an impregnable city, strengthening it with earthworks, traces of which remain, and with pallisades, of which only the name is left. The eleven thickly wooded acres which had held Ethelfleda's strong city of Eddisbury, still retain the title of the Old Pale, and the "old farm-house" Muriel was about to visit, dated back to times when Delamere Forest was a chase for the ancient Earls of Chester, and the chief custodian of the red and fallow deer held the so-called Chamber of the Forest, with a band of subordinates to assist in the maintenance of the forest laws, and his own privileges. This was even before James the First knighted the Chief Forester, or confirmed the appointment to Sir

John Dene and his heirs for ever, and so the Forest House towards which Muriel was wending, had, like the forest itself, seen its palmy days depart, and was not merely old, but ancient. But paint and whitewash covered up the wrinkles of time, and it still showed a good front to the world from that coign of 'vantage, "the storied hill of Eddisbury."

Nothing of this had floated into Muriel's dreams, when she was startled from a doze by the return of her Uncle Sam and his exclamation, "No sign of dinner yet, and two o'clock! It seems there are some fine folk upstairs, mother, who came in yon chaise before the door, and there's been such a fuss made over getting dinner for them all in a hurry, that plain tradesfolk that travel on horseback must e'en be content to wait. Oh! you're here at last," he cried, as the hostess herself came in close at his heels to lay the cloth, and apologise for keeping old customers waiting; but "the lady who came in the yellow chaise," she said, "was ill, and sick folk must be minded first."

"So they must," assented Mrs. Bancroft, "and I've been in no hurry. I wanted this little lass to have a good spell of rest before her dinner."

Muriel was too much shaken to eat a good dinner, she felt as if all her bones had been dislocated; the hour's rest had not refreshed her much more than the repast; but she was unwilling to cause unpleasantness or disconcert her grandmother's arrangements, so, when the meal was over, she answered Samuel's "Well, are you ready?" with a smile and a prompt assent, and stifled a sigh of weariness as she stepped up on the horse-block, to resume her seat on the pillion, well repaid by her grandmother's look of satisfaction; though if she had obeyed her own inclination, she would have preferred to stay where she was.

She was aware that Mr. Kingsley was the Chief Forester of Delamere, and that her grandmother, who had large dealings with him, carried a silver whistle in the shape of a horn, which had been given to her as a token, but until Uncle Samuel had spoken she had no idea they were going to the Forest House. It was a relief to learn they were not going on to Chester that afternoon. And Sam was in haste to get to their journey's end before dusk, as the road was not too lively, and not in too good repute.

Mrs. Bancroft had a small freehold property at Waverham, on the north-east border of the forest, which required her supervision, and for this, and other reasons, she had set out a full fortnight before Michaelmas, and a week prior to the fair. A few days later the road would be alive with travellers of all sorts and conditions wending towards the same goal. As it was—though the post-chaise had left the inn not ten minutes before themselves— only a stray pedlar, a labouring man, children nutting or blackberrying, or a farmer on horseback, were to be passed upon the road; and when once they were fairly in the forest, notwithstanding the clearness of the afternoon and the mellow tints of the autumnal foliage, there was a sharp breeze which swept the deep waters of the meres into mimic waves, rustled over the waving fronds of fern, went singing and sighing through the trees, driving the brown and yellow leaves in showers around them, and somehow revived the mysterious influence of the old tales she had so often listened to at home.

Yet as they rode steadily and slowly along the ascending road, past wide stretches of boggy moss, or yellow broom, undulating pasture, billowy brake or low copse where trees were sparse, her mind was disabused of the idea that a forest was a dense impenetrable mass of trees, such as she had read of in an old book at home, King Arthur and his Knights of the Round Table sought adventures in. Still there were giant oaks, and stately elms, and graceful birch, and smooth-boled amber-tinted beeches massed together here and there between, and in the distance might wooded Eddisbury be seen like a dark cloud of firs against the opaline sky. And as high overhead a pair of wild ducks took their flight from mere to mere, or a crested grebe on whirring wing obeyed the

call of an expectant mate, or a frightened hare
or rabbit scuttled away for safety amongst the
herbage, or a solitary lapwing trying the speed
of its thin legs against their horses', broke the
stillness with the sharp " peewheet, peewheet "
of maternal care; all these sights and sounds
unwonted told the town girl they were
intruders on nature's domain ; and that where
was a covert for deer was a covert also for
men of evil deed, and evil fame.

She clung closer to her uncle in silence, not
because he was a favourite, but because she
was timid as well as tired ; and as they passed
moss and mere, she scarcely heard her grandmother whilst pointing to places on their route
say, " That's Massey Lodge," " This is Crab-
tree Green," " Yon's the Plague Hole, where
the dead were buried," and so on, for very
weariness and apprehension, not allayed when
Samuel Bancroft—who could feel her trembling even through his thick riding coat—in a
spirit of mischief pointed with his whip ahead
to their right, with the remark : " And yon-
der's the Thieves' Moss. Muriel. It lies in the

corner where th' roads meet." Was not the very name significant?

If in her unselfishness she had complied with her uncle's wish, and ignored her own fatigue rather than be a cause of expense and delay to her grandmother, she began to think it might have been as well to have accepted her kind offer and remained at the inn, and to fancy the afternoon was closing prematurely, and that a robber was lurking behind every tree and bush.

All at once, as if it had been whispered in her soul, came the recollection; "Mother has often said father was as safe in the forest as in the town if God's angels had him in their keeping;" and there was strength in the inspiration, not of body, but of mind. The road was too rugged and uneven to let the body rest.

They skirted the moss with the evil name until the Chester road was crossed by another which led uphill to the dense woods of the Old Pale, where was situated the Forest House whither they were bound. Here they turned at a sharp angle, still keeping the Thieves' Moss to their right, and had gone several paces forward when something like a scream broke the stillness.

Horses and riders pricked up their ears. Muriel's heart stood still.

"It is only an owl," cried matter-of-fact Samuel. "Let us get on."

"I tell thee it's a woman," insisted his mother. "We'd best see into it," as a second and more terrified scream, blent with a confusion of sounds, came in confirmation on the breeze.

Without waste of words mother and son turned their steeds back, and after a moment's deliberation urged the tired beasts along the winding road towards Chester. In less than three minutes they sighted an overturned chaise, to which the restive horses were threatening destruction, obviously the one which had been re-horsed in Northwich, from its conspicuous yellow body and the luggage strapped behind.

"Oh! the poor lady!" cried Muriel, her

dread of robbers vanishing before this real disaster. "And I'm sure she was ill. I saw her face as they drove off."

In another minute they were on the spot, their bridles hitched to a bough, Samuel cutting away at the traces with his clasped knife and shouting to the postillion to keep his plunging horses steady. Mrs. Bancroft's ready hand unfastened the door of the upturned chaise, and a fine man in military undress, whose right arm was in a sling, struggled forth with her aid.

"I thank you, madam," said he with the politeness of habit; "but oh, my poor wife and son! I fear they are killed!" and as he spoke in tones of deepest emotion he bent to look within the chaise, and called anxiously, "Celia! Arthur!"

"*I* am not killed, sir," answered a voice from within; and as the head of the speaker, a handsome youth of sixteen, emerged from the vehicle, Muriel clasped her hands in a tremor of shuddering dismay, for a line of blood ran from a wound down the side of his face. "I was only stunned, sir; but I fear my mother is more seriously hurt. She is quite insensible. Will some one assist me to raise her?"

Samuel Bancroft stepped forward. The horses were cut loose, and the postillion kept them aloof, but the chaise was a wreck, the officer disabled, the lady to all appearance dead or dying, and the evening closing in.

"What *is* to be done?" ejaculated the gentleman in trouble and perplexity, without any hope of a solution.

"I'll see to that," said Mrs. Bancroft briskly, as she withdrew her head from the chaise. Up to her lips went the silver whistle slung from her neck, and at once over moss and mere, brake and thicket, went out a quick succession of throbbing notes clear as the ring of a bugle, and echo seemed to catch up the tones and send them back from near and far; and presently, as if in answer to the call, along the rutty road, over the dusky sward, forth from copse and woodland, one figure after another loomed dimly through the mist and came towards them at a run.

At the first note of the whistle the officer had started in apprehension. "Was this break-down a plot to rob them, and this hard-featured woman in league with highwaymen?" he thought; but he cast his eyes on the pitiful face of Muriel, and was reassured.

Mrs. Bancroft had seen his startled look, and answered it. "Eh! we are peaceful travellers, sir; you need not be alarmed. I carry this whistle as a safeguard, for I have been hard beset in this forest myself before now. It was the gift of the head forester, and here come the keepers to protect or assist their master's friend."

One by one as the men came up, each, armed with gun and hunting-knife, doffed his cap to Mrs. Bancroft, as if in respectful recognition.

The situation was apparent enough. Samuel Bancroft and the youth between them had with some difficulty managed to extricate the lady from the broken chaise, and on its cushions, placed by Muriel on the grass by the roadside, she lay with her eyes closed, still insensible, her husband bending over her and Muriel chafing her small white hands as a restorative, her own face pale as that under the hood of the injured lady.

Mrs. Bancroft and her son held a brief conference with the keepers. The officer was spoken to.

The postillion rode back ruefully to Northwich with orders, not merely concerning his carriage, but to offer a heavy fee in the name of Captain Wynne, of the Royal Welsh Fusiliers, to a doctor to stimulate his speedy attendance at Eddisbury.

The captain stripped off his crimson scarf of netted silk with the remark that he "never thought it would be put to such sad service," and it was spread to form a litter for his wife, whose only sign of life was a quiver of the nostrils, a momentary raising of the eyelids when Samuel Bancroft poured a few drops from his spirit flask between the white lips.

The captain's son, though he had made

light of his own injuries from broken glass, was not sorry when Muriel offered to bind up his bleeding head, and Mr. Bancroft passed the flask to him, with the hint "you had better mount Ball and take charge of my niece. You don't seem in fettle for a long walk."

The luggage was unstrapped, and mounted on broad shoulders; but as there were four or five keepers, and Mr. Bancroft offered to lend a hand at the litter, one of them set off by a short cut to apprise Mrs. Kingsley of the coming guests, expected and unexpected, and the procession moved forward as quickly as care would permit; Captain Wynne by the side of the litter with his wife's hand in his own; Mrs. Bancroft riding in advance and keeping her eye not so much on steady-going Ball as on his new rider, behind whom Muriel had been mounted.

She was afraid lest he might faint and lose his seat from loss of blood, and bring Muriel down with him; but of any connection between the handsome young stranger and her grandchild beyond the courtesy and service of the hour, she had not a scintillation in her brain.

As for Muriel, she was in the sight of Arthur Wynne just a good-natured, tender-hearted child who had done what she could for himself and mother, the mother whose peril absorbed all his thoughts and interest; and Muriel's too, for that matter. The untoward accident had put shyness and timidity to flight, and called forth all the pitiful tenderness of her nature; personal fear and fatigue were forgotten, whilst anxiety for the strangers amongst whom she had been thrown blent with rejoicing that she had not yielded to her own sense of weariness at Northwich, and so detained her grandmother.

Mist rising from mere and moss had met the descending twilight, blotting out the brushwood and the road before them; but the veil on the forest path was not so deep as that which hid the future path of life from all.

CHAPTER IV.

AT THE FOREST HOUSE.

WHEN Sarah Bancroft said "I'll see to it," discussion was at an end; she had put down her foot, and opposition was useless. It had been so in her brief married life, and in the long years of her widowhood. It was so in her household, and in her business. When she said a thing must be done or undone, it was so. When she named a price to give or to take, there was no chaffering, no argument. It must be or not be. When she had said "I'll see to it," Ellen D'Anyer knew that her daughter was to all intents and purposes taken from her. Mrs. Bancroft's "I'll see to it," meant that she had taken Muriel's future into her hands, as if she had the power and prescience of Deity.

It was true she had done this in the very plentitude of her love for the girl, for, as her son Samuel knew full well, Sarah Bancroft had warm and susceptible pulses in her breast, though her sharply outlined features bore false witness against it, and she covered up and hid her affections out of sight, as weaknesses to be ashamed of, and kept well under control; as her dominant will kept all around her.

She had never reasoned the matter with herself, but that she was born to rule she had never a doubt, any more than of her own infallibility. She would have acknowledged a Supreme Ruler had the question been put to her, but no one put the question, and she felt herself sufficient for all things. Her faith was in herself—to herself she was a law. When Captain Wynne's troubled exclamation was answered by her decisive "I'll see to it," and she raised the forester's silver whistle to her lips, it was as though an imperial fiat had gone forth; a guarantee of safety and protection, care for the sick lady, hospitable welcome for all. *She* had so decided, and who should demur?

Certainly the keepers looked one at another, but no one disputed her behests; and if Captain Wynne took all for granted and was profuse in thanks, and Muriel never doubted her grandmother's power and prerogative, Samuel Bancroft did.

He knew that Mrs. Kingsley was an Arden, and never forgot for how many successive generations an ancestor of hers had been "Chief Forester and bow-bearer of Delamere," and that she never allowed her husband to forget that it was in *her* right he held the office, even though the Kingsleys had held it first of all. And he felt pretty well assured that no silver whistle would have been granted to his mother without Mrs. Kingsley's full concurrence; but he was equally sure she never contemplated its use in the service of casual wayfarers, and felt somewhat dubious of their reception.

He was right. The furrier's party had been expected, and for them hospitality had provided its best. But for any additions to that party in the shape of strangers pulled out of a broken-down chaise the forester's wife was not prepared—and not disposed to prepare. For once Mrs. Kingsley's insulted dignity overshadowed her humanity.

"What! bringing a flock of strangers into this house without invitation or permission!" she exclaimed, as the keeper delivered his message. "Does Mrs. Bancroft mistake the Forest House for her own, or for an inn?"

"I think, wife," said Mr. Kingsley astutely, "Sarah Bancroft just took thee for what thou art, a kind-hearted, hospitable woman, too good a manager to be put about by two or three extra visitors, and too good a Samaritan to let a fellow-creature perish by the wayside."

"Indeed!" was all her response, though she muttered to herself "Surely the inn at Kelsall might have served their turn." Her husband's two shots had failed to bring dignity down from its perch, and she lost sight of humanitarian necessity in her desire to teach Sarah Bancroft a lesson.

A large wood fire was blazing and sputtering on the stone hearth in the large square entrance-hall, where stags' heads and antlers were interspersed with other trophies of the chase—bows and arrows, hunting-whips and horns, fowling-pieces and shot-belts, as decorations on its walls of pannelled oak, with a primitive oil-lamp or two on brackets to show their glories off. A carved oak settle and its table, with a few straight-backed oaken chairs, ranged against the walls, were all the furniture, but two great hounds lay basking before the fire on a deerskin rug, and the atmosphere was redolent of venison and hare and other savouries.

The wide door stood open, the light streamed a welcome out to friends and to strangers ; the Chief Forester pressed forward to greet the former and to give hospitable assurance to the latter ; the very dogs rose from the hearth to salute the new-comers ; but Mrs. Kingsley, in her green silk quilted petticoat and overgown, stood frigidly apart with folded hands, to mark her sense of the intrusion; and for once Mrs. Bancroft found her sagacity and sufficiency at fault.

Even Captain Wynne saw there was some misunderstanding, and pressed forward to apologise; but Mrs. Kingsley chanced to catch a glimpse of the pale face of the lady in the litter as she was borne in and laid on the oaken settle, and of the stained bandage above the equally pale face of the youth by her side, and all her womanly sympathy was aroused on the instant.

As she approached the litter she answered the apologist, to the utter exclusion of the others, "I can understand, sir, you were misled; but be under no concern for this lady, she shall have every attention, although this is *not* an inn, and the influx of so many guests was not anticipated." Then with the same unwonted loftiness, turning her head, "Mrs. Bancroft, I trust you are willing to surrender *your* room to the lady *you have brought?*" and she laid an emphasis on the closing words.

"Of course I am, or I should *not* have

brought her here. And I brought them all here on the strength of your hospitality and goodness to me on a like occasion when I was a stranger. If I've made a mistake we can settle it afterwards."

And there is no question that they did settle it together afterwards; but for that night Mrs. Kingsley was on her mettle to prove herself a good hostess and a kind nurse.

Muriel might have been unnoticed amidst it all had she not followed Mrs. Wynne's bearers up the stairs and along the gallery which overlooked the hall, to the ready chamber, her weariness forgotten in her desire to be of service, and taking Mrs. Kingsley by surprise by her aptitude and readiness in administering such restoratives as were at hand, and her delicacy of touch whilst helping to disrobe the lady, whose wrist was injured, and hung helpless.

And what a bright face was hers, when she bore the intelligence to the anxious father and son, "Mrs. Wynne has come to herself, and asked for you." Who then observed that it was seamed and scarred? Had not her glad tidings irradiated and beautified her countenance? Did she not seem to them one of the good angels that walk the earth in disguise?

Something of the kind glanced through the mind of Mrs. Kingsley, when Muriel, perceiving how she was distracted between her duties as hostess and her cares for the invalid, volunteered to remain with the sick lady until the doctor came, so that others might go in to supper.

"I can attend to Mrs. Wynne by myself; I am not afraid, and I am not hungry," she said, adding, "and the doctor will surely be here soon."

Mrs. Kingsley had certainly been troubled about the long-delayed supper and the spoiling viands, but as she went across the wide gallery and down the broad oak staircase, she thought to herself what a patient little maiden she had left behind in the big bedroom hung with tapestry, and full of flickering shadows, as the firelight rose and fell without reaching its remote corners.

And some remark of the kind she made as she took her place at the long table in the dining-room on the right of the hall, which had been set more than an hour with the whitest of home-spun napery, the brightest of silver tankards and Sheffield cutlery, and where drinking-horns with silver rims flanked the horn-hafted knives and two-pronged forks instead of glasses.

"As composed and observant as a woman," she said, "and not at all afraid to be left alone with Mrs. Wynne, in that strange room, away from us all."

"She was timid enough as we came through the forest," interjected Samuel Bancroft, with something like a grin; "I've a notion she fancied there was a robber hiding in every bush."

"Then thou hadst frightened her!" said his mother across the table, "and there was no need of that: she had heard of Delamere before to-day."

"Hidden dangers are apt to impress the imagination, sir," put in the captain, resting his fork; "I have known men who never blenched before the fire of the enemy, shrink from the shadows of a dark room; the little lady must be naturally brave."

"She removed a splinter of glass, and bound up my head, without any show of either fear or repugnance," added the captain's son.

"She seems a born nurse," then said Mrs. Kingsley, as though in praise, as she helped Samuel to a second slice of venison.

"A born nurse! I hope she was born for something better!" quoth Mrs. Bancroft, bridling. "I'll see that Muriel D'Anyer is no nurse."

"I think you misunderstood, madam," the captain began.

"Oh, no! I did not," she answered. "I'm taking her——"

But the doctor—whose name was Holmes, a little fat, pudgy, round-faced man—coming at that instant, the rest of Mrs. Bancroft's speech was lost.

The captain was too anxious about his wife to continue at the board, and though with an ill-grace at the interruption, Mrs. Kingsley held him excused.

Mrs. Wynne was discovered to be suffering from a broken wrist, and from severe shock to her system, already enfeebled.

"She will not be in a fit state for removal for many days, and will require the utmost attention, if she is to be removed at all. But she is in good hands."

So said the doctor; but he knew nothing of the irritation of Mrs. Kingsley at having the patient thrown on her hands in such a matter-of-course way, to say nothing of the additional husband and son; when she had calculated on a long gossip with her old crony.

Good part of the forester's income was derived from his perquisites in the matter of skins, and his wife's indignation at the use Mrs. Bancroft had made of the silver whistle, intended as a safeguard to herself, had annoyed him greatly, Mrs. Bancroft had bought so largely from him. He was a good-natured fellow, and was pleased at supper-time to find that matters had adjusted themselves comfortably.

Judge then his annoyance when Mrs. Kingsley broke in on a business conference in the malodorous skin-store the next morning, with Mrs. Bancroft and her son, just as the prices and quantity of deer, squirrel, marten, and fox-skins had been settled, and the question how many hundred hare and rabbit skins should be supplied at a given rate was under consideration.

The morning opinion of the Northwich doctor had been promulgated, and Mrs. Kingsley came, in anything but the best of humours, to vent her indignation at being "saddled with the care and cost of an invalid and her relatives, for no one knows how long."

"Would you have had the poor woman die in the forest?" asked Mrs. Bancroft.

"Certainly not!" was the tart reply.

"Then be as thankful for the chance of saving *her* life," answered the other, "as you were when you took charge of me, and as for the cost——"

"Why, make a bill out, and ask the captain to settle it," thrust in Samuel, who had always an eye to the money; and thought that a very plain solution of the difficulty.

Mrs. Kingsley drew herself up, and her nose curled: "As if we were innkeepers," said she.

"Here, Mr. Kingsley," said Mrs. Bancroft, "take your whistle," and she released it from her neck. "You'd best have it back, as I don't know when to use it. Sam, go and see the horses saddled, we'll be off to Waverham at once. And we'll take Muriel with us. If we're not expected till to-morrow it won't matter much there. But before we go I'd better seek out the captain, and let him know that I've made a mistake for once in my life; and *I'll* see about hiring a nurse in Waverham, if there's no objection to *that*."

And off Mrs. Bancroft set towards the house, greatly to the chagrin of both Mr. Kingsley and his wife, who followed her with entreaties to return. He was afraid to lose a good customer, his discomfited spouse to have the truth blurted out to Captain Wynne all too bluntly. She was not an unkindly woman in the main, and had grumbled more to "put Sarah Bancroft down," than from any lack of Christian kindness towards the sick stranger.

Samuel slapped his thigh in satisfaction as he looked after them from the door of the outbuilding—a place fitted with louvre-board windows to admit air. "Egad, Mistress Kingsley is caught in her own trap now! I'd back my mother against her any day! But I must be off after the horses if she's made up her mind to go." Then he stopped short, and as if he had hurt his thigh in slapping it, rubbed it slowly and ruefully. "Whew!" he half whistled to himself, "suppose we're in th' wrong box in Waverham too; an' it's like enough if Lydia's none prepared. It's awkward anyhow," and he went on his errand slowly enough.

Captain Wynne was found pacing the stone

floor of the entrance hall, his left hand supporting the arm in the sling, shaken when the chaise overturned, his head down, his mind a chaos of anxiety and perplexity. The precarious state of his wife; the wound in the head of his son, which threatened to prove troublesome; his own helplessness, the result of a duel with a fellow-officer, were sufficient causes, without the consciousness that they were trespassing, still further to chafe the proud man, who was accustomed to command and to control; and found himself cast like a straw upon a stream, through the mere loosening of a linch-pin.

He had entrusted to Mr. Holmes, the surgeon, who had undertaken the charge, money and a letter, to be despatched posthaste to Chester for his own servants. They had been " sent on as couriers in advance to have all things prepared at the Blossoms Inn," he said, " and would be themselves uneasy and all at sea."

The announcement of Mrs. Bancroft's sudden departure took him by surprise.

Somehow, though she did *not* suggest it, he felt answerable for the change in her plans. He had, whilst pacing to and fro, observed Mrs. Kingsley intercept Mrs. Bancroft in a side passage, and hold her as if in argument, where the former seemed to urge and the other unwilling to comply.

"I am convinced we are trespassing here," he said, as both women came into the hall together, "yet with my poor wife's life hanging on a thread I see not how it is to be remedied. What compensation I can make to our excellent host and hostess for this intrusion on their privacy, and to your little grandchild for her tender ministrations——"

"We seek no compensation," began Mrs. Kingsley loftily.

"My grandchild's done her duty, Captain Wynne, and that's her reward," interrupted Mrs. Bancroft stiffly. "But Muriel's going, and I came to ask if I had not better hire a nurse in Waverham, one you can pay out of your purse, and who can wait on Mrs. Wynne night and day."

"Miss D'Anyer going? I'm sorry for that. My son, who is upstairs with her and his mother now, tells me that she is the tenderest of young nurses, one of the sweetest creatures that ever entered a sick room. I am sure my wife will miss her greatly. I should say that I have already sent to Chester for Mrs. Wynne's own maid, but if—of course with Mrs. Kingsley's sanction—you do not mind the trouble of finding a suitable attendant, you will add greatly——"

"If my servants and myself are insufficient, you are at liberty to do as you please in sending for your own, Captain," interrupted Mrs. Kingsley; "but don't you, Mrs. Bancroft, send Maggy Blackburn into *my* house," and she turned on her heel as if she considered the proposition a fresh indignity.

Now Maggy Blackburn was precisely the nurse contemplated by the furrier, but though a skilled attendant on the sick as times went, and a village doctress of more than local repute, she had two not over reputable sons, men suspected of a liking for game and other property not their own—they were in very ill odour at the forester's.

There was a window with a wide seat at each side of the entrance; into one of these the captain flung himself as the very sport of fate, bitterly lamenting the mischance of the broken chaise, nay even the humiliating intervention of Mrs. Bancroft—and she was on her way upstairs to summon Muriel to depart, when in through the passage burst Mr. Kingsley, his brown face lit up with excitement.

"I say, Captain, you may thank God your chaise broke down when it did, and that the Bancrofts were at hand to bring you here!"

"Indeed!" interjected the captain in a tone not altogether free from incredulity.

"Aye, that you may! A traveller was plundered and wellnigh murdered by two ruffians last night—not half a mile farther up the road."

"Hah!" cried the officer, with amazement on his face.

"He was speechless," continued the forester, "when one of our keepers found him there battered and bleeding, with his pockets inside out. And it was all Whitely and another man could do to get him to the inn at Kelsall. He had come to himself before they left him, but I hear he's in a bad way. He must have had a horse, for he had a whip in his hand, but the horse was gone. Helped the foot-pads to make off, I reckon. *You* had a narrow and most providential escape."

A providential escape! and he had been questioning the ways of the Most High, as he had chafed and fretted in his walk on that stone floor. A providential escape indeed! A mercy not to be forgotten!

"We may indeed be thankful," he said seriously. "But cannot something be done for the injured traveller?"

"Well, I'm just off to see what can be done for him, and who he is. A man with empty pockets is like to find cold comfort at an inn. Though he might be worse off than where he is."

"I shall be glad to bear you company, sir,"

then said the officer to the forester, "and to hold the innkeeper indemnified in case the poor fellow be unable to pay. And if you will allow me—I should like to reward the humanity of your keepers. I owe them something on my own account."

"Tut! Tut!" said the other as a put off, but Captain Wynne was not a man to be put off.

The news spread quickly. Not one of the travellers but felt there was an escape to be thankful for.

"I expect that break-down was planned," said Samuel; "I half fancied the rogue of a postillion was playing tricks with his horses, and now I am sure of it. My hat to a button if that chap was not playing into the hands of the robbers. Belike going shares!"

"Robbers! then there were robbers after all!" cried Muriel, clasping her hands when she heard. "Oh, how glad I am that we did not stay in Northwich! and that grandmother had that whistle! Oh, Mr. Arthur, if robbers had attacked you it would have killed your mother with the fright, ill as she was! God's angels must have been around her," and she looked reverently up.

"I think they *were*," said he; but he knew not she referred to her own mother's words, and his had a double signification.

Mrs. Kingsley summoned one of the keepers and questioned him; and in the general excitement Sarah Bancroft's departure was retarded. Indeed to travellers like herself, a violent act of highway robbery such as that was not to be disregarded. She was anxious to learn more, and that prompt measures should be taken to discover the criminals and bring them to justice. And the exciting question was still under discussion when Mr. Kingsley and Captain Wynne returned. The latter much agitated.

"My God! Arthur, what do you think? The poor fellow lying there disfigured and lamed is Norris!"

"Norris?" ejaculated the son in a higher key, "What brought Norris there?"

"Owen's over-anxiety and his own fidelity.

They became alarmed when we failed to arrive in the afternoon. At last he mounted and left Chester to meet us. Their idea was that your mother was too ill to proceed; and that his services might be needed. Poor fellow, he has paid dearly for his zeal. The miscreants struck him from his horse, and then rifled his pockets. There was very little worth taking, except his watch, and in their rage they beat him unmercifully. He will never be good for anything as a soldier again!"

"And his horse, Captain," put in Sam, from the oaken settle, " was that worth much?"

"Worth something as a horse, sir, worth nothing in the calculation of loss, where a faithful servant's life is concerned," was the answer, which somewhat took Mr. Samuel aback; at least he rubbed his knees, and said no more.

Then Captain Wynne expressed his hope that Mrs. Wynne should not be disturbed with the intelligence.

"I think you may trust Miss D'Anyer for that, sir," said his son.

"Miss D'Anyer will not be here, sir," observed Mrs. Bancroft stiffly, once more adjusting her cloak, and making a move.

"I say, you'd best take the whistle back, Mrs. Bancroft," suggested the forester.

"Aye, and make yourself comfortable where you are," added his wife, more ashamed of herself than she liked to own. "Miss D'Anyer has seen nothing of the place yet, and I'm sure she will not want to go whilst Mrs. Wynne is in danger, besides I don't think she could be spared, she is such a helpful little body," she was going to add, "and such a capital *nurse*," but she remembered the grandmother's indignation at the word, and stopped short in time.

The forester joined his wife in her arguments, and after some little persuasion, to which Sam added an interested word, Mrs. Bancroft, for a marvel, yielded to persuasion, took back the whistle, the horses were unsaddled, she completed her purchases and orders; and when she and Samuel started for Waverham the next day, Muriel was left behind, to her own satisfaction and that of others.

Mrs. Bancroft had seen a finger that was *not hers* directing these events, and pondered over it. But she did not take the lesson very deeply to heart; and went forth on her other errand to control human lives and destinies, as if she had a right Divine.

CHAPTER V.

RED RIDING HOOD AND HER FRIENDS.

MORE than a week had gone by, a week which Muriel devoted to the sick lady, with the solicitude of genuine interest, without asking herself how her services were regarded, or to be requited. She was one of those who could not witness suffering without an active desire to alleviate it, one whose simple aim seemed to be to make herself useful to others.

It was nothing to her that Mrs. Wynne accepted her ministrations as one accustomed to homage and attention, one whose patrician birth entitled her to such service as her inferiors were ready to render. And if Mrs. Wynne considered the child honoured in being allowed to wait upon her, had not Muriel said the same, and meant it.

What knew the lady of the long passages and flight of stairs Muriel trod up and down so frequently on her behalf? or of the wearisome watch in a darkened room, when the sun was shining on the autumnal foliage without, and the twitter of birds, as well as the voice of Mr. Kingsley, tempted the town girl to stroll with him and Arthur Wynne through the enchanting woodland? Was it not sufficient that she, the daughter of a baronet, recognised the peculiar delicacy of Muriel's touch, and preferred her attendance to that of Mrs. Kingsley or her own maid, Owen, who was now by her side? And when at length able to recline on a couch by the wood fire, was it not enough that she smiled on the gratified young nurse and pressed into her hand a locket rimmed with gold and pearls, in which reposed a coil of her own auburn hair?

Proud indeed was Muriel of the delicate lady's progress toward recovery, and said it; proud too of the souvenir so earnestly pressed upon her; but had she or Sarah Bancroft either had an inkling that the crystal locket with the jewelled rim was tendered as *payment* to cancel an obligation, the one would have laid it down in sorrow, the other flung it back in scorn.

Captain Wynne had chafed under the obligations pressed on him by circumstances, as such, but he had the sense to see the spirit in which services were rendered, and that in their degree the Kingsleys and the Bancrofts were every whit as proud as himself, and he was careful not to wound a feeling he understood.

He was liberal to the two keepers whose humane attentions to Norris had kept life in the man, no less than to those others who had rendered him and his personal service, but he saw intuitively that the Kingsleys would be insulted by offers of repayment, and his proud spirit chafed at the dilemma in which he was placed. His own sense of justice told him that he had no right to trespass on the hospitality of strangers; yet here they were quartered upon civilians for an indefinite time, and civilians who assumed the rank and position of equals. It was a trial to the pride and independence of the military man, and he paced the long stone hall by the hour, inwardly rebellious and annoyed, outwardly reserved and silent. In his manner when addressed he was courteous, gratefully urbane—but there was an evident effort to keep irritation down, and he was not cordial.

The young man alone (after the feebleness consequent on loss of blood had worn off, and he was no longer compelled to lounge in an easy chair by his mother's bedside, or on the oak settle in the great hall) fraternised with their hospitable entertainers, made friends first with the hounds, then sought initiation into the mysteries of woodcraft, and was equally ready for a day's jaunt with Mr. Kingsley, taking the inn at Kelsall by the way, to look in upon Norris, and see that he was not neglected, or for a day's sport, and bore the forester company with such an easy acceptance of the situation as put those around him at their ease also. Certainly *he* was at the age of adaptability.

He had insisted on Muriel, whom he had dubbed " Little Red Riding Hood " from the scarlet cloak she wore, joining in a stroll through the park of the Old Pale and over the slopes around Eddisbury on the day before her departure.

"You may safely leave Mrs. Wynne to Owen's care now," he said, "and I am quite of Mrs. Kingsley's opinion that you have been too long shut up with our invalid. A ramble through the woods will bring your roses back; and I will take care no wolf runs away with you."

"Ah," she answered with a smile, "the wolf did not run off with Red Riding Hood from the wood. It was in her grandmother's cottage he ate her up; there are no talking wolves now," and clasping her cloak she stepped out of the doorway with him, as he replied,

"Don't be so sure of that, Miss D'Anyer, there are talking wolves to be met everywhere, but they go on two legs, not on four. I've heard it was a wolf of this description set his teeth in my father's arm." And the young man's face clouded as he spoke.

"A wolf!" she echoed incredulously, "I heard your father tell Uncle Samuel that he was wounded in a duel. But perhaps you are right, for I think men who fight duels are worse than wolves, and worse than Cain, since they go on purpose to murder one another, and I do not think Cain knew what he was doing. *He* had never *seen death* before he struck his brother."

Arthur Wynne looked down at her in amazement. "That is a new doctrine," he observed gravely, after a pause, "I shall not forget it," and for some time he walked on in silence, keeping the child's hand in his as an elder brother might.

It did not strike her that she had reflected on his father, and if it occurred to him, he made no remark.

Presently she stopped and looked back at the house, with its many angles and gables, its black beams intersecting in strange devices the weather-stained roughcast, its windows of all sizes, from the tiny dormer to the broad mullion, and the one fine oriel over the entrance, from which the road swept downwards in a steep but gradual descent. It had been a noble edifice in its time, but its best days were gone, and there was a portion lapsing into utter decay.

"I wonder how old the Forest House is?" soliloquised Muriel as she scanned it thoughtfully. "It looks older than grandmother's houses in Toad Lane, and they have been built hundreds and hundreds of years!"

"We want my uncle, Sir Madoc Wynne, here to settle that question," replied Arthur; "I am not much of an antiquary, I only know that the place is very ancient. Mr. Kingsley tells me that Eddisbury was a fortified city in Saxon times; his own and his wife's ancestors have held the place as Chief Foresters since the twelfth century."

"That is a long time," said Muriel, "it tires one to count back."

"Aye," responded her companion, "it is almost as far back as Sir Madoc counts the pedigree of the Wynnes."

"Pedigree! Oh! that's what my father talks so much about. And it is *so* tiresome. I don't think a long pedigree makes people kinder or better. Do you?"

"I have not considered the question, I will tell you when I do," and he laughed lightly, showing a set of firm white teeth, and then he stopped, and pointing westwards bade her "look across to the far horizon. You see those gray mountains standing up like clouds against the sky? Amongst them lies the home of Sir Madoc and his ancestors—and mine," he added as an afterthought.

"And that shining like water with the sun upon it, and those church towers?" she asked, as if not much interested in ancestry.

She was told she looked on the river Dee and Chester's old cathedral and churches; but there was a wide and varied landscape spread out before them, nearer Oakmere glittered like a diamond amongst emeralds, and from another point in their ramble came Halton Castle into view with the river which gave its name to the ancient kingdom of Mercia; the river which had scarcely begun to swell with its own importance, for the merchant-fleets of the Mersey were then unbuilt.

It was all new and glorious to Muriel, her brown eyes expanded to take in the panorama of moss and mere, village and woodland, city or stream or mountain, and then as they strayed through the woods tinged with the gold and brown of autumn, or on the grassy upland, the young man and the child, she filled her hands with flowers, nor questioned how many might have kept possession of the soil since Saxon spades upturned it, though every blossom called an exclamation forth. Tangled amongst bushes and brambles (with the blackberries of which her mouth and fingers soon were stained), she found the white and rosy trumpets of the bindweed, in shady nooks the hart'stongue fern, and others of the tribe; Scotland's emblem, the spear-thistle, held its head erect, and braved the gatherer, but she did not despise the yellow corymbs of the common ragwort, or the golden disk of the dandelion; she found too a single raceme of the pure blue milkweed, and another blossom of the eyebright, lingerers from July; and out in the open, a nodding harebell and a tuft or so of flowering grass were added to her posy, of which she was not a little proud.

It was shown with delight to Mrs. Kingsley, who, thinking little of these wild natives of the forest, smiled at the girl's simplicity, yet supplied a queer-shaped vase of antique ware to hold them. And then they were carried as a precious gift to the invalid, on whose lips came a suspicion of a faint curl as she barely glanced at them; but Owen bade her place her bouquet on a table in the oriel, and there they were left, to be ignominiously cast out on the morrow, when the giver was herself gone, as " disgusting weeds."

But the harebell and the eyebright were not thrown away with the rest. Someone had taken them from the jar; someone who had pleasant associations with the "vanished hand" that had culled them; someone who could symbolize the graceful form, and the bright eyes of the unsophisticated child with these wildlings of the wayside and the wood; someone who had learned a lesson from the child of which manhood might need a reminder.

"Well, have the murdering ruffians been caught yet?" were the first words of Mrs. Bancroft as Mr. Kingsley helped her to dismount the following morning, when she and her son came for Muriel. "Has the captain's good horse been recovered?" was the question of the latter.

"Neither," was the answer of the forester. "But there are two men missing from the forest, who were hanging about the day before; and the captain's gone to Chester to set the hounds of justice on their track."

"Aye," chimed in Mrs. Kingsley, "and we've a notion Maggy Blackburn knows more of the business than an honest woman should."

"What, Nurse Blackburn?" and a curious look crossed the face of Sam Bancroft as the ejaculation escaped him.

"Aye, Nurse Blackburn!" quickly responded the mistress of the Forest House, with a look as curious and meaning into the calculating eyes of the querist, which shifted beneath hers, "she's none too good, if all were told; and she knows many a thing more than she tells."

"Hush, hush, wife, a still tongue makes a wise head, and Maggy Blackburn's not to be blamed for her lads' misdeeds."

"I'm not so sure of that, she should have brought them up better."

"So she should," echoed Sarah, with a proud glance at her own son, as much as to say, "See how he has been trained." "As the twig is bent the tree inclines."

"Is Muriel ready?" interrupted Sam, who had his own reasons for changing the subject.

"Yes, here she comes," cried Mrs. Kingsley, as Muriel at that instant crossed the gallery at the far end of the hall, in her scarlet cloak, with the hood well drawn over her gipsy hat, whether for riding, or to shadow eyes moist from parting with languid and feeble Mrs. Wynne it would be hard to say. "But you won't go without a bite or a sup, and dinner on the table ready for you."

Sam excused himself on account of the horses standing out in the cold, but their host set his mind at ease respecting them, and soon he was busy with the game-pie and the home-brewed, talking politics with the forester, whilst his mother between the pauses of knife and fork had a private gossip with Mrs. Kingsley.

Muriel had been called to the board, cloaked though she was, and young Mr. Wynne, who had her flowers in his button-hole, saw that she was not neglected.

After luncheon there was another run up-stairs, for another good-bye of Mrs. Wynne, Mrs. Bancroft following her grandchild, and both wishing the lady a speedy restoration to health, for which she thanked them condescendingly, with the graceful langour of excessive debility.

But no sooner had the door closed behind them, than the sensitive lady cried to patient Owen—" My salts, Owen, my salts! How that horrid old woman smelled of cheese! And, Owen, bathe my temples with the Hungary water, her loud coarse voice has distracted me. Thank Heaven! they're gone. That child's exuberance had become quite oppressive. And," after a pause, "my good Owen, when you go downstairs, don't forget to throw out those disgusting weeds."

But when Muriel had taken leave of his lady mother, Arthur Wynne accompanied her to the front entrance, and with much real friendliness lifted her to her seat on the pillion behind her uncle, whilst Mr. Kingsley, as of old, helped Mrs. Bancroft into her saddle. He had a grateful heart, had the young man, and saw that in his mother's set phrases of farewell for which he would have been glad to make amends.

On the broad doorstep, beneath the oriel, also stood Mrs. Kingsley, in a figured linen morning gown, whose last words were, "You will let Miss D'Anyer come and spend her holidays here, old friend; my young folk will be home then, and they will show her about. She has seen nothing of Delamere yet, mewed up in a sick room," apparently forgetful that Arthur Wynne was present, still pale, and with a plaistered forehead, but courteous and gentlemanlike as his father, for whose temporary absence he had thought fit to apologise, not omitting thanks in that father's name, and his own.

"I'll think about it," was Mrs. Bancroft's brief response to the invitation, as she stooped to exchange a last business word with Mr. Kingsley, whose hand was on her bridle.

But a smile of truthful earnestness broke over Muriel's homely face and lit up her expressive face while she answered for herself: "Nay, I had a delightful walk through the woods yesterday, and I am sure I have altogether had a very pleasant visit."

"You have done your best to make it so for others, Red Riding Hood," observed Arthur Wynne, as he shook hands with her a second time; "I do not know whether my mother will miss you most or myself, and though we may never meet again, I assure you, I shall always remember the cheery little maid with the gentle fingers and compassionate brown eyes under her red riding-hood. I shall have a reminder here," and he touched his wounded brow; "Good-bye!"

"The war-path and the trade-path do not often cross," murmured the young man to himself as the travellers rode off, Muriel nodding back. "There is not much chance of *our* meeting again. D'Anyer! I wonder how she came by her aristocratic name. By the way, she said something of her father's pedigree. I'll ask the forester. Anyway she is a most obliging creature! I wish I had a sister like her, though she is not handsome. There is something in those brown eyes that is better than beauty. I would my father had been here to take leave of them. I am afraid my mother does not sufficiently estimate our obligations to little Red Riding Hood and her friends, and he does."

And now the travellers from Manchester were again on their road, each carrying away a new chain of associations and speculations.

If Sarah Bancroft's equanimity had been disturbed at Eddisbury, it had been restored at Waverham; and as for her son, why, he carried satisfaction under his three-cornered hat and buttoned up under his dark long-tailed riding coat if any one did. He had persuaded his mother that she was arranging that which *he* had arranged and settled quite two years before, and he had done it to his own satisfaction.

"Yes, Mrs. Kingsley, Sam is to marry Lydia Bradley at Christmas; it was that which took me to Waverham this time," Mrs. Bancroft had said to the forester's wife before she came away. "He has loved the lass many a year, but he has stuck to his mother and the business, and would not even ask the girl till I had seen her and said I was willing. Not like that daughter of mine, Muriel's mother, who took the world on her shoulders at sixteen, with never a word to kith or kin. No,

I told Sam to see and keep single, and he has done so to please me, and now I mean to take him into the business, and find him a house to live in, and the farmer will fit up the house for them. I've settled it all."

"Ah, well, it's about time Mr. Samuel had a home of his own and a wife in it, and Lydia's a notable body," observed Mrs. Kingsley dryly, asking after a pause, "Shall you come for the wedding?"

"Nay, it's our busy season, they can wed without me."

"So they can," assented Mrs. Kingsley with a secret undercurrent of silent ejaculation. "Bless my soul, how clever people can be taken in! Trust Sam Bancroft to get all *he* wants!"

And having a prospect of getting all he wanted, even to a share of Farmer Bradley's guineas, Samuel chuckled at his own cleverness as he rode along; and cracked sly jokes with the people on the road, for now there were many journeying to the fair.

Muriel knew nothing of the business which

had taken them to Waverham, or of the coming marriage of her bachelor uncle; and as they jogged along her thoughts went back to the Forest House and those she had left there, and lingered amongst the rustling bracken or the many tinted bushes, followed the flight of waterfowl from the meres, or of a hare or rabbit as it scampered out of sight, or travelled ahead to Chester Fair and the unknown school where her journey was to end.

Daylight had not touched the veil of dusk when Boughton Road was left behind, and Foregate Street rose on either side, quaint and curious. Midway, Sam made a feint of stopping; he pointed to an opening on the right, "Here's Queen Street, mother; suppose we leave Muriel now."

Muriel's heart gave a leap;—surely she would not be left among strangers so abruptly!

"Ride on, lad, and no nonsense," said her grandmother, and speedily, to Muriel's relief, the horses were entering the city under the wide arch of the East Gate, and picking their way amongst a throng of people and horses and vehicles, and stalls of all kinds and degrees, from that of the itinerant quacksalver to that of the respectable tradesman.

For although there was a ground set apart for the purposes of the fair, it was pretty much abandoned to dealers in horses and cattle, the booths of travelling showmen and mountebanks; and the absolute buying, selling, and barter of merchandise was carried on in the highways and inns of the quaint old city. The church of St. Peter had already hung out the symbolic white glove, and the fair was declared open.

It was not altogether a novel sight to Muriel. Manchester had its fairs, if they differed somewhat in character and importance, and also had its narrow streets of overhanging timber houses, picturesque and diverse of gable and tint; it was only when she saw the people walking in the Rows in an arcade above the lower shops, or leaning on the parapets, and amongst them Welsh-women with men's beavers above their linen caps, that a feeling of strangeness was aroused.

So slow was their progress amongst the crowd that she had ample time for observation, and she was scanning curiously the Yacht Inn at the corner of Nicholas Street, where the ground floor modestly retreated into the shade, and the upper stories advanced successively overhead—quite unconscious that they had halted at the old commercial house, or that the red-faced landlord was waiting to lift her from her seat—until she had a hint from her uncle.

"Come, Muriel, lass, bestir thyself. What art' dreaming about?"

They were shown into a low-ceiled apartment where candles were already lighted, and tables were spread with comestibles for the influx of customers peculiar to fair time. Huge loaves and joints of meat which had lost their fair proportions, remnants of pies, the separate halves of a cheese in japanned biggins, and these flanked with mugs of brown stone-ware with a foam atop, or brightly polished tankards of ale. But Mrs. Bancroft was disposed for something warm after her journey, and soon a tea-board was before her, and as she poured out the fragrant beverage for herself and Muriel, Samuel carved a roasted capon, and dispensed it with the savoury adjunct of broiled ham. But he preferred a pull at a tankard to sips at a tea-cup.

Muriel's appetite, as before, had been jolted out of her.

"You'd best make a good supper, lass," said her uncle, as he laid down his knife and fork, and smoothed his hands along his thighs. "There's no knowing when you'll have another. They'll not feed you with fowl and ham at school," and he chuckled until he choked.

Muriel looked alarmed.

"Be quiet, Sam; don't you scare the lass!" put in his mother sharply. "She will have plenty of good wholesome food. I'll take care of that. Do you think Miss Briscoes would have such a name if they starved their scholars? You might delight in tormenting her!"

Whether or not, he had put to flight what

little appetite Muriel had sat down with; and sent her to bed in very unusual depression.

She was, however, fresh for breakfast the next morning; and when that meal was disposed of, was in hopes that her grandmother would take her to the fair. But no, Mrs. Bancroft was too keen a business woman to waste a morning so unprofitably. She did not mean to be unkind, but hers were trading instincts, and Muriel *there* was an encumbrance.

I'll see about it before the fair's over. You may look about you as we go along. I've already given a week to the king, it won't pay to throw another day away into the bargain," was all she said as she took Muriel by the hand and stepped on briskly towards Queen Street.

Samuel had been off some time to look after their furs and peltry at the new Hall and to see it unpacked.

CHAPTER VI.

LEFT WITH THE MISSES BRISCOE.

THE highly genteel residence of the Misses Briscoe, was a solid if somewhat grim brick building with stone dressings, and a flight of steps the iron handrails of which swept outwards with a curl right and left.

There they were shown into a fireless reception room painted brown, where a pair of globes stood sentry in arched recesses on either side the hearth, and spindly fire-irons in tall rests within a perforated steel fender had an air of never being used, any more than the square footstools on either side, where a worsted cat and dog preserved unbroken peace. High backed chairs, with contorted limbs and painted velvet covers, were ranged like a regiment against the sombre walls, whereon hung the pictorial embroidery and poonahpainting which was the school's diploma; and on the centre table were books and other nicknacks presented by grateful pupils or their friends.

After waiting a few moments the two Misses Briscoe entered together, the thin mittened arm of the one sister resting on the thinner mittened arm of the other. Their high heeled shoes fell on the faded carpet in precise step, and their tall caps and prim long stomachers seemed to bend in unison as they courtesied with gracious if formal politeness and smiled urbanely. They were supposed to confer a favour in accepting the pupil.

Brusque Mrs. Bancroft was not easily overawed. She had no time to spare for ceremony, and after introducing Muriel as the Miss D'Anyer about whom she had written, plunged into business at once.

The two maiden ladies, nowise disconcerted, shook Muriel by the hand, spoke to her with reassuring gentleness, told her she need not tremble, she was certain to be happy under their auspicious guardianship; rang the bell for a "Miss Williams," and desired that young lady, with the most benignant of smiles, to introduce their charming new pupil to her schoolmates.

As a rule, Muriel was not demonstrative; but then, notwithstanding the winning aspect of the teacher and the honeyed words of the Misses Briscoe, she flung her arms around the neck of her grandmother, and as if struck with a quick foreboding, cried piteously, "Oh, grandmother, dear grandmother, do not leave me here; take me back to my mother; take me back to my mother!"

"My dear, you are disturbing your kind relative; pray control your emotions," said Miss Briscoe calmly, releasing the clinging arms with prim decision, and leading the young girl to the door and to Miss Williams, as if the latter had been a sort of warder and she a captive; her grandmother's "Don't fret, Muriel, I'll see you again before I go back," following her with just a gleam of comfort.

There was a slight twitching of Sarah Bancroft's hard mouth and a suspicious moisture in her eyes as Muriel was led away, but Miss Briscoe's unruffled demeanour recalled the business woman to herself, and she soon found that the Misses Briscoe, although smooth and velvety as peaches, and she as rough as a russet apple, were traders as keen and astute as her own self.

There were so many small matters to be paid for, not mentioned beforehand as extras, so many little items in the way of plate and linen to be provided for the pupil—and left for the school, so much to be settled and arranged respecting course of study and needlework, the use of harpsichord and library, each meaning a fresh dip into the pocket. She, however, was prepared to be liberal, and only stipulated that Muriel should "have a sound education, plenty of good food, and a comfortable home."

Alas for fair promises and testimonials! The Misses Briscoe traded on their power to mould their pupils to pattern, their own frigid gentility the model. They made too much of their Christian principles, and were strict observers of fast-days and forms. But what hearts they might have had in their youth, had shrivelled up like their lean bodies; and the human hearts and souls in their charge were all but ignored in their system of training and discipline.

They had a single parlour-boarder, and for the first fortnight Miss D'Anyer was permitted to take her meals along with this privileged young lady, at the table of the Misses Briscoe, which was set forth with due regard to the proprieties—and economy. But no sooner was the fair over, and the Bancrofts and D'Anyers "gone beyond come again," than she took her place with the rest of the pupils.

True to her promise Sarah Bancroft had not only obtained the Rev. Thomas Bancroft's promise to watch over Muriel, as she told her for her comfort before she went away; but she had also called to see her grandchild and take her round the city, and although Miss Briscoe and her echo had done their polite best to convince her that "Miss D'Anyer was perfectly happy, and that it would be a thousand pities to unsettle the dear young lady again," she said she "would rather risk that than break her word."

She tempered her abruptness with an invitation for Miss Briscoe to join them, and then there was no longer any demur.

With a face all smiles, her scarlet cloak around her shoulders, her gipsy hat tied down under her chin, Muriel would have rushed to her grandmother's embrace, but there was a restraining hand to intimate propriety. And there was the chilling presence of Miss Briscoe, with eyes and ears open, whether under Mrs. Bancroft's guidance they traversed the Rows, or the walls, that enclosed the city within a quadrangle of defensive rampart which peaceful citizens had converted into a pleasant promenade. And whether proud of her native city, or of her historical lore, the precise and stately preceptress descanted learnedly and loftily as they went—if somewhat parrot-like —on its glories and antiquities, ignoring, if not ignorant of the fact that Sarah Bancroft knew pretty well as much of Chester as she did herself, and most likely would have told her so, if Muriel had not been there to see and be instructed.

She, poor child, would much rather have cuddled up close to her grandmother, on this last day, and have talked of her mother, and George, her father, and her sisters, and her cousin Milly Hargreaves, but politeness condemned her to listen, and ere long she found herself interested. For though she did not care to hear that the citizens owed "to the noble house of Grosvenor the magnificent new arch" of the Eastgate (by the steps of which they had mounted to the walls), and could only see in the Cathedral an enormously big church rather out of repair, when they reached the angle of the wall where stood the Phœnix Tower with the canal flowing tranquilly beneath, and was told that "during the memorable siege of Chester King Charles the First looked out from the top and saw his troops defeated by the Parliamentarians on Rowton Moor," she seemed to feel for the sorrow of the poor king; and would fain have gone herself to the top of the tower and have looked out like him, but her companions scanned the formidable ascent to the doorway and the promise of further steps inside, with wholesome regard to their own years, and breath, so Muriel scampered up the steps alone, to be recalled midway, with a quick "Miss D'Anyer!" in which was compressed the essence of the censure and rebuke she would have in full the next day.

She had scarcely forgotten her own disappointment, or that of King Charles, when they reached the old North Gate, where their path lay under a narrow arch in a superincumbent pile of buildings, dark and ancient, the roadway of course running under the larger arch below. Here Miss Briscoe made a pause to be the more impressive.

"This," said she, "is not only our North Gate, but the City Gaol, and is of most renowned antiquity; indeed its foundations were laid by the Romans. Of course *I* was never inside," and she drew herself up virtuously, "but I understand it contains some curious cells, and instruments of torture such as were used in the old days of religious persecution."

"They don't use them now, I hope," put in Muriel earnestly.

"Oh, no, my child, those dark ages are past, no one is tortured now-a-days. There was a meddlesome fellow, called John Howard, who has a mania for visiting prisons, came here five years ago and he reported that in this City Gaol, the convicts and prisoners for trial, were severely ironed by the neck, hands, waist and feet, and chained to the floor, and at night to their beds in the horrid dungeon; and he also said that the 'allowance of a pennyworth of bread for felons, and a pound for debtors, was inferior in quality to that sold in the city.' And many other things he said, even that 'men and women were not properly separated;' all reflecting on the humanity of the gaoler. But no doubt he exaggerated grossly; or if not, does he expect that we are to pamper criminals? If men will commit offences, or will not pay their debts, they deserve to go to gaol. They have no one to blame but themselves if they are punished."

"I don't think they have a right to put fetters on a man before he is tried," was the commentary of Mrs. Bancroft who had a habit of forming her own opinions, though not more inclined to deal leniently with offenders than others of her age and time.

But Muriel, who had listened with dilating eyes, broke in breathlessly:

"I don't think they have a right to put anyone in irons, and chain him to the floor; I think *that* must be torture."

"Little girls of your age have no *right* to think," was the severely grave rebuke of Miss Briscoe, and Muriel was silenced.

Then, as if to efface any impression of harshness she might have left on Mrs. Bancroft's mind, this inimitable trainer of youth waved a thin arm and a yellow mitten with a courtly air, towards an old building in an angle of the wall, with the gracious intimation, "And now we approach the 'ancient hallowed Dee,' as the poet Drayton designates our classic river, and here stands the Goblin Tower; the Watertower you may observs lies down below, though the water no longer washes its base as of old."

Her hearers followed the wave of her arm, and looked out over the flowing river and the wide expanse of country on the other side which Mrs. Bancroft told Muriel was Wales; but she was impatient to get back to her business, and Muriel had not overcome the impression made upon her by the shadows of the dark Northgate, and John Howard's report thereon. Her heart ached for the poor prisoners confined within those hard stone walls, and she saw and heard all else vacantly. The word *Wales* somehow brought up other associations, and she wondered if the men who had robbed and beaten Captain Wynne's servant would be put in that "horrid dungeon," and chained to the floor if they were caught, and with a child's logic began to hope they would not be caught, if that was how they would be used—though they did certainly deserve punishing.

Her grandmother observed that her mind was astray, and asked "What art' a dreaming about, Muriel?" and being told, answered, but not harshly, "Don't thee bother thy young brains o'er such things, lass! Rogues like those deserve hanging, and nothing less. How else are honest folk to travel in peace?"

This was another problem for Muriel, who walked dreamily on over the Watergate and past the Roodee, and only roused when the Castle was pointed out.

"What! a real castle where knights in armour used to live and fight!"

The exclamation was addressed to her grandmother, but Miss Briscoe replied:

"Yes, Miss D'Anyer, and the ground at the end of Queen Street, where you saw the shows and mountebanks, was formerly the 'Justing Field,' where the armed knights were wont to 'tilt.'"

"Oh, like Prince Arthur and Sir Lancelot du Lake, and Sir Tristam," and Muriel, who had met with a few old romances, glowed with a new enthusiasm.

"I'm afraid, Miss D'Ayner, yours has not been an improving kind of study. We must amend that," and the enthusiasm was damped.

Indeed, whenever the natural girl broke forth, or addressed herself to her grandmother, or crept to her side lovingly, there Miss Briscoe interposed to keep the palpitating young heart within bounds, and repress any undue confidences. And when, having left the Bridge-gate far behind, and the Wishing-steps which promise so much that can never be, and having made the circuit of the walls, descended once more into Eastgate street, Miss Briscoe retained Muriel's hand within her own; "for her safety in the throng of the fair." Nay, even when Mrs. Bancroft led the way to the New Manchester Hall, and generously pressed upon the admiring schoolmistress a mink muff and tippet each for herself and sister, with a view to bespeak favour for her grandchild, her vigilance scarcely relaxed.

It was during the selection of these that Muriel saw her father for a moment, but he was busy with a Welsh customer bartering fustian, tufts, and moleskin for flannel, and had not even a kiss for the child, who sighed and watched him wistfully, but beyond a brief "Good-bye, be a good lass," she had no further word or speech from him.

"Do not disturb your good parent, you see he is engaged," had been Miss Briscoe's frigid reminder, unheard by the grandmother, or she would have set that matter right.

With half-closed eyes Samuel Bancroft had " taken stock " of the stately old lady as she entered the hall in the wake of his mother, and courtesied to him as formally on introduction as if in a drawing-room, and he certainly must have sent a random shot home to *her*, when he saluted the girl in his idea of jocularity with, " Well, Muriel, you're a prisoner now, I hope you like your gaolers."

He had the jocularity taken out of him, however, before the day was two hours older when someone came to talk to him about prisoners and gaolers, a tall thin woman in a grey cloak, whom he called "Maggy," and who came with a request, which took the form of a demand, a demand that had to be complied with before he got rid of her.

It must have been no joking matter to him, for long after she was gone, he looked right and left and rubbed his knees, ejaculating under his breath, "Egad, its well that antiquated piece of frozen honey and vinegar took our old dame out of sight and hearing, or there'd have been the very devil to pay."

It might be well for Sam, but though her grandmother went back to Queen Street, and she was politely invited to take tea at the same table, Muriel had not one moment's private speech with her.

The wary spinsters might have spared their pains. Muriel was not given to feel oppressed, or to complain; they checked some loving messages home, but no undue revelations. In fact she had hardly bent her shoulders to the yoke of discipline when her grandmother went; but with the closing of the door began her school-life in earnest: school-life as it was in the last century, when even in the home the birch was the symbol of rule.

She had her first shock on the night of her entrance, when the bedfellow to whom she had been assigned, a Miss Alice Ford, from Northwich, led her upstairs to the dormitory which she was to share with several others.

It was not only that there were five or six pallet-beds in the room, or that pillows and coverings were scant, or that she objected to a bedfellow, or to wash in a basin of water common to others, or that the dim rays of the dip-candle, placed on the landing to serve four rooms, had a struggle to reach her corner, or that she was told she must have her clothes folded and be in bed in less than ten minutes; it was the culmination of all these in a babel and a scramble in which there was no pause for prayer, in which she knelt down amidst confusion, to rise from her knees in the dark, which seemed to overturn all her own mother's reverent teaching, and overwhelm her with dismay.

CHAPTER VII.

MURIEL'S NEW LIFE.

FROM a confused dream of home, and of nursing her infant brother, whose crying was not to be stilled, Muriel was aroused at six the next morning by the loud clangour of a bell. There was a general leap to the floor, and a repetition of the overnight scramble, not unmixed with contention who should be first to use water or towels, whose turn it was to fasten the backs of bodices, or to make the vacated beds, the prompt willingness of Muriel to give place or to assist others resulting in disaster.

When the bell rang its second summons her frock was not on her shoulders, and of those she had been ready to help not one would stay to fasten it for her. They could cry, "Make haste, you'll be late!" but only

Miss Ford, the daughter of a Northwich yeoman, had the grace to turn back and bestow three minutes on the new pupil.

Those three minutes represented a reprimand, and a fine which went into a money-box "for the poor." No excuse was admitted. Miss Ford paid for her act of courtesy (on the score of dilatoriness), and once more Muriel's sensitive heart was shocked. That she, being fresh to the school, and ignorant of its rules, was exonerated, was no satisfaction to her so long as another was punished on her account. She would have refunded the fine.

"Keep your pence," said Miss Ford, who was two years older than herself; "you will need all your pocket-money."

And so Muriel thought when Miss Williams warned her not to stand on the hearth or she would be fined, and when the entrance of Miss Betty after a tour of inspection in the dormitories, and the discovery of stray articles, such as caps and brushes, added sundry pence and halfpence to the growing fund "for the poor."

Whilst Muriel was speculating on the sum in the box, and the amount so collected in a year, Miss Briscoe appeared, and bent her head with a formal "Good morning, ladies," as her sister had done, to be in turn saluted with low and elaborate courtseys from the pupils *en masse*. Miss Williams, the mild and ladylike teacher, then placed a large book on a table near the fire, and at the signal, with wondrously little shuffling, the girls dropped to their knees simultaneously, and Miss Briscoe read, or declaimed, a morning prayer from the volume.

After prayers there was more reprimanding for inattention, carelessness, lack of devotion; and Muriel wondered at her own escape, for her mind would stray homewards, and institute comparisons between the prayers of her mother and of Miss Briscoe.

Breakfast followed, but until she had ceased to be the especial guest of the principals, Muriel knew nothing but hearsay of schoolroom fare.

Her first experience was of the boiled milk

and bread set before the young ladies for **breakfast** thrice a week, which the careful cook had seasoned with bits of egg shell, cheese, suet, etc., shaken in with the crumbs from the bread-basket and kitchen table. "Oh! for a cup of the new **milk** from the Stocks' Farm, and a plate of oatmeal porridge! This **mess is** uneatable," thought she.

There were plenty of hungry candidates for **that** which she rejected, and on milk mornings she generally went breakfastless.

Nor did dinner make amends. A good appetite **was** "vulgar," "over-feeding tended to corpulence," consequently the meat and vegetables were doled out with due regard to the slim gentility of the young ladies. The consternation when "Oliver Twist asked for *more*," **could not** exceed that when Muriel **passed her** plate innocently for "another potato, if you please."

As at dinner, so was the long tea-table set out, with due regard to gentility. Each young lady had her own china cup and silver spoon; but **a very** wishy washy apology **for tea** was poured therein, and *one* tiny lump of *loaf-sugar* duly dropped in from silver tongs as flavouring, by Miss Williams, who presided. (Brown sugar was not genteel, and white was expensive.) Plates of thick bread, with a microscopic film of butter, were ranged at intervals, and hungry Muriel unsuspiciously helped herself to more than the regulation quantity.

Some one else, better informed, must have done the same, for when Miss Ford and the other monitress, whose duty it was literally to *wait*, sat down to their own chilled repast, the plates were bare.

"Oh, that's nothing new," was the answer of her next neighbour, to a question from Muriel; "only two pieces each are sent in. If any one takes more, some one must go without. There is no more to be had."

Muriel was dismayed. A second time Miss Ford was doing penance for her. She could not stand that. Her sense of justice overcame timidity. She rose, and begged that

Miss Williams would order in a fresh supply, explaining that she found she had taken more than her share.

"It is against the rules," said the teacher quietly, but she flushed to the roots of her hair, as if she felt her task unpleasant, knowing how insufficient was the quantity for growing girls.

It is certain that Muriel's frank admission and request were not displeasing, or she would not have shut her ears to the indignant "It's a shame!" with which the novice sat down. As certain as that Muriel had a friend in Miss Ford from that hour.

And it was no unusual thing for kindly-disposed Rachel Williams to close both her ears and eyes, when by so doing she could ward off punishment for trivial offences. How else would it have been possible for the day-scholars to smuggle in the buns and rolls half-famished Muriel and her companions gave them the secret pence to buy?

She had a gentle heart, and had been tenderly nurtured, but her mother had long been dead; her father, a naval officer, had fallen in battle, and she was dependent on her situation for support. Many were the indignities she herself bore, and bore calmly, waiting patiently for the day in the unknown future when her lover, a Lieutenant Grifliths, in her late father's ship, should come and claim her. Not that she was altogether friendless; she had an aunt in Wales who would have made a home for her, but self-respect inclined her to turn her English education to account, and to put up with minor evils philosophically. She saw much in the fashionable boarding-school which she was powerless to remedy, but she had the consolation of softening asperities, and even of turning hardships to a Christian account.

Muriel soon learned to look to her for counsel and comfort. After carrying her silver-clasped Bible to St. John's Church a couple of Sundays, it was coolly transferred to Miss Briscoe's hands, and not returned. "It is too costly for a child's use," she was told. The girl felt as if a portion of her heart had been torn away, yet she could not venture to expostulate. To Miss Williams she went in an agony of grief, and laid bare all her mother's wishes, and her own promises, as bound up in that volume, and her dread lest it was gone for ever, and the fulfilment of her promise with it.

"My dear Miss D'Anyer," said the teacher kindly, making the best of what she disapproved, "do not be alarmed! When you leave the school, your Bible will be restored to you. No doubt Miss Briscoe considered that the parade of so costly a book before your schoolfellows was calculated to arouse pride in yourself, envy and other ill-feelings in them. You would not wish to tempt others to evil. Consider it as a temptation out of your way; and remember that your promise to your good mother was made as a means to build up a Christian life. I will find you a plain Bible and Prayer-book, which will serve that purpose quite as well; and I will give you what help I can—a quiet half-hour now and then, for reading, and explanation when any difficulty arises, if you will regard me as a friend."

Muriel could but remember, as the explanation so kindly put made itself felt, that she had indeed been proud of her exclusive possession, as if it conferred distinction on herself; and she recalled too the upturned noses of her schoolfellows; their nods, and looks, and sly nudgings as she had taken her place in the file, book in hand; to say nothing of the whispers.

"Isn't Miss set up?" "Silver clasps indeed!" "Vastly fine!" and other sneers which had reached her in passing, and being open to conviction, she grew calmer as she listened to Miss Williams' apology, if not altogether reconciled to her loss.

It was soon buzzed about that Miss Briscoe had impounded the coveted volume, and then the same young lips twitted her spitefully with the "pride that had a fall," until Miss Ford interposed between the passive Muriel and their ill-nature.

She soon found that the teacher was as

good as her word. Without the slightest show of favouritism, Miss Williams made her feel she *had* a friend beside her there; and truly a friend was needed to make the strict routine endurable. Not that it was worse for Muriel than for others, only that she was sensitive and susceptible.

So much time was given to study and needlework, so little, so very little, to recreation; unless the hour devoted every morning to deportment was considered such. Muriel did not think it very lively to bend her knees in courtseys till they ached, or to be screwed up in the stocks to turn out her feet, or to march about the schoolroom with a leather collar propping up her chin, and her arms pinioned by a backboard to improve her figure. She would much rather have walked up and down the kitchen at home with George in her arms, or led a game of romps with her younger sisters, and I am afraid was not over grateful to her grandmother, whose motives had not been confided to *her*.

Yet it must not be forgotten that for

healthful exercise—and the parade of the school—there was the weekly promenade round the city walls, with the favour of an occasional detour into the Rows, when those whose pocket-money had not already gone in secret to the baker's, or openly to the poor-box, might regale at the pastry-cook's, and lucky did the girls think themselves if now and then the Misses Briscoe delegated their guardianship to Miss Williams and a monitress.

Muriel would have considered herself fortunate had it been so on that brisk December day, when she had been ten weeks in the school. Instead, Miss Briscoe, stiff as any other martinet, marched at the head of the graduated file of girls, whilst Miss Betty brought up the rear. Miss Williams was a prisoner to the schoolroom, keeping guard over lesser prisoners then in disgrace.

It was a very staid and decorous but not very animated procession. The keen air sharpened appetites already sharp enough, and the cold pinched fingers and toes already in danger of chilblains. Muriel was well protected from the weather. Other girls had muffs, or cloaks, or gipsy bonnets of straw, but her bonnet was a glossy black beaver, roughened by every breeze, and worn in conjunction with muff and cloak, the combination brought her into trouble. They had not proceeded far in their routine walk along the walls, when, midway between the Wishing steps and the Bridge-gate a young lieutenant of the Royal Welsh Fusiliers, was observed lounging idly against the parapet. He had a handsome face under his black cheese-cutter hat; and as his scarlet coat and white spatterdashes set off a well-formed if slight figure, no wonder if more than one stray glance went towards him.

All at once he gave a recognising start, ejaculated "Red Riding Hood, by all that's wonderful!" and, with a well-pleased smile breaking over his face, darted forward and offered his hand to Muriel, who took it, nothing loth, and answered his "Miss D'Anyer, how glad I am to see you!" with "And so am I, Mr. Arthur. But I did not know you. I hope Mrs. Wynne is better, sir."

"Ah the hair-powder and uniform disguised me, I suppose. Now it was your familiar attire caught my eye! Oh, thank you, my mother is——"

He got no farther. Miss Betty from the rear, and Miss Briscoe from the van, had come aghast to the rescue. Consternation sat on every youthful brow but Muriel's, and she wore a look of questioning perplexity. With awful severity Miss Briscoe demanded,—

"How dare you presume, sir, to accost one of *my* pupils without sanction? Lying in wait to arrest her progress during our promenade! It is monstrous!"

Lieutenant Wynne bowed, offered a deferential explanation and an apology; but Miss Briscoe was not to be mollified, or misled, as she phrased it. "Your colonel will hear of this matter, sir," was her final and decisive blow.

Arthur Wynne raised his hat, bowed regretfully, said to Muriel, "I hope, Miss D'Anyer,

I have not plunged you into disgrace with my precipitation," and stepped back, leaving the way clear.

But the scandalized spinsters were so much discomposed by the pouncing of this wolf in uniform on one of their flock, that nothing but immediate return was possible. It was only in the security of the haven in Queen Street that they could deal with a matter of so much moment. The very character of the school was in peril.

As for Muriel, solitary confinement and bread-and-water diet for the remainder of the week was her portion. Her attempt at explanation only made the matter worse. "Not known him a fortnight! It was disgraceful!"

Solitary confinement in a fireless room in midwinter with such dietary would now-a-days rouse the indignation of parents, and drive the educational professor into the Bankruptcy Court. Then, it was a part of the common system, and it was not for the pupil to rebel or the parent to remonstrate. Alike in our army, our navy, and our schools, discipline was preserved rigorously.

If Muriel, catching at a word thrown out by the young officer, whose commission was little more than a month old, looked for the appearance and intervention of Mrs. Wynne, she was disappointed. That lady never came, although her health was sufficiently re-established for visiting.

"The schoolmistress was quite right, Arthur, and most discreet," she had said to her son, "You certainly took a liberty."— "Yes, gratitude is vastly proper, no doubt, but it has limits and degrees. Mine does not prompt to a cultivation of an acquaintance with a school-girl, or her trading relatives."

Captain Wynne must have thought somewhat differently, since, before Miss Briscoe could forward her complaint to the colonel at head quarters, she had a visit from him. He came less to tender an apology for his son than to inquire for Miss D'Anyer, and to smooth away any misconception by the remark that he and his were under considerable obligations to the young lady and her friends, and he desired to thank her in person. Yet so little deference did he pay to Miss Briscoe's dignity, and so little was she disposed to admit precipitancy or mistake on her part, that the captain was constrained to take leave without seeing Muriel, and the message he left was never delivered.

But such a flutter had the officer's arrival created, that the news went to Muriel as a " profound secret " along with her bread and water.

For a moment it warmed up the chilly atmosphere of her dormitory; but it passed, and added only one more to the many problems her child-brain attempted to solve during her fasting solitude. At first she had flung herself down on the deeply recessed window-seat, and coiling her pinafore round her bare arms, looked down vacantly on back-yards, where garments from the wash alone enlivened the scene, and on the playground where was never any play, wondering and pondering the nature of her offence.

"Oh, what would I not give for my cloak, or my fur muff and tippet, from the robing-room!" she murmured to herself, as the cold seemed to freeze her blood; "I dare not wrap myself up in one of the quilts or they would chastise me as they did Miss Sims. It is very cruel! I wonder if either Miss Briscoe or Miss Betty was served so when they went to school! But what *is* it all for?" And then she walked about the long room to keep herself from freezing utterly; still turning over and over in her mind the injustice of her punishment, the hardship of her daily life, the stern discipline of the school, her grandmother's motive for singling her out for such an experience, the pain it would cause her mother to know what she had to endure, the wonder no letters came with home news or inquiries, the aching fear lest she was forgotten; and then with the memory of the Sunday evening sermon at the Octagon Chapel, came the inner questioning if she was expiating some unremembered sin; and the preacher's category of "sins of omission," coupled with his fiery denunciations, filled her with terror.

Unknown to all, Muriel passed through a crisis of her life in those three solitary days. There had been bitter moments when there was danger that her soft and sensitive heart would harden to stone under the sense of neglect and cruelty. But on the eve of the second day (the day on which Miss Ford, as monitress of her class, brought up on a daintily covered waiter, the bread and water for her mid-day meal, and with it the secret of Captain Wynne's visit), whilst the Misses Briscoe were sipping their souchong in contentment, Miss Williams, whose heart ached for the innocent offender, carried her own tea up to the bewildered pupil sitting alone in the cold and dark, and with it, a downy angola-shawl of her own; determined to brave the censure of her employers if it came to their knowledge.

"Here, throw this over your shoulders, my dear, and drink this tea, it may serve to warm you," was all that she said, but it was sufficient. Muriel knew instinctively that the tea was her teacher's own, that she would herself have to go without, and that simple act of self-denying sympathy turned the whole current of the girl's feelings. She burst into tears. The teacher had to slip back hurriedly, but she had time for a few words of healing, and when she left the crisis was past. Muriel sank on her knees and prayed. It was a child's prayer; but it went up to heaven on the wings of faith and submissive humility.

The learning of a psalm had been part of her *punishment*; the Bible left with her for the purpose became an up-springing fountain of *consolation* for her all the last day of her penance, and for ever after; and she gathered strength from it as well as comfort and guidance. That which had been intended by the Misses Briscoe as a *penalty* for speaking to a stranger, and which had called up a spirit of rebellion long dormant, was, with God's blessing and the kind teacher's instrumentality, converted into a permanent benefit. Whithersoever Miss Williams went, went also the Three Christian Graces, and she had introduced them to her sad little friend.

All the school was agog the following week. Letters were to be written home. It was a sad damper to the uninitiated to find they had to be draughted on their slates, and to be submitted to Miss Briscoe for revision and interpolation before they could be transferred to paper. Muriel's epistle had undergone wonderful transformation in the process, and she felt some compunction in setting her signature to it when complete.

"How am I to sign this? It is not true," whispered Muriel across the double desk to Miss Ford who sat opposite.

"What *you* wrote was true. Leave the alterations on Miss Briscoe's conscience," was the cool reply, and after a little more hesitation the letter was signed.

The answer came in a hamper just before Christmas time, when the other pupils were looking forward to home cheer and festivities. Muriel did not see it opened; but Miss Briscoe reported among the contents three letters,—

one for herself and two for Muriel, two books, and a large currant cake. This she was at once allowed to cut up and distribute amongst her companions. Then, and not before, Miss Briscoe *read out to her* slowly and deliberately, as if she were picking her way amongst the words and sentences, that which had been penned by her mother and grandmother for the girl's own eye and heart, and to which Muriel listened with clasped hands and eager eyes.

They were just such letters as might be expected to answer her fabulous epistle home. She was congratulated on her health, her happiness, her attachment to her benign teachers, and was told to be thankful for a home so replete with comforts denied in other schools which they could name. Then followed the home news, and this swallowed up the advice with which the letters were concluded.

She learned not only that her Uncle Sam was gone to Waverham to be married to Lydia Bradley, but that her little brother George had been dead for more than six weeks,—the brother she had nursed, who had learned to walk by her hand.

After that Miss Briscoe's dry, hard tones fell on deaf ears. Muriel sat on the form with her hands still clasped, but as one crushed and stunned. There were pitying glances directed towards her, but she seemed neither to hear nor see. At length Miss Williams took her by the hand and led her to her own room, where the sluices of grief might open and relieve the bursting child-heart.

She did more. Under the conviction that it would be cruel to leave the young thing with those frigid spinsters in that great house, alone with her new sorrow, she obtained permission (granted readily enough on the calculation that her board would be saved) to bear Muriel away with her to Wrexham, where she always spent her own holidays, at a large farm about a mile beyond the town, with her good-natured and hospitable Aunt Parry.

CHAPTER VIII.

MRS. HOPLEY'S POSTSCRIPT.

ONLY three weeks' holiday! Yet what a boon and a refreshment it was, alike to worn-out teacher and pupil. To Muriel it was nothing less than a providential change for which soul and body were the better.

Fancy what she would have endured shut up for those three weeks with the prim and unbending spinsters in their formal back sitting-room, without recreation or books calculated to dissipate her new sorrow—the library of which she had " the use " was scant and heavy—or waking the echoes in the solitary dreariness of the uncarpeted school-room and dormitories; to pass and re-pass servants to whom she might not speak; to shiver in view of a fire she might not approach; and to sit in silence at a precise table where her portion of food was all too meagre.

And then contrast the untrammelled freedom of the farm-house life, which she had been so fearlessly invited to share, and where a hospitable welcome met them in advance with the farmer's cart at Wrexham, to be repeated in every act and word of her kind hostess. True, everyone there save Mrs. Parry had a Welsh tongue, and her English was none too fluent, but Miss Williams was a ready interpreter, and in her absence a smiling pantomime did duty for speech ; and it was good fun for Muriel to pick up words and phrases in the Cymric vernacular. Then there was the abundant and nutritious fare—milk, eggs, poultry, apples, honey, without stint, with the very sweetest of brown bread and butter.

Muriel had learned to milk at the Stocks' Farm. It was a renewed pleasure to pat the sleek sides of the small Welsh cows, and try her hand afresh at milking time. She could help to feed the poultry, watch with interest the processes of churning, butter and cheese-making, and could share in the Christmas merry-making, where the strange costume and speech were part of her entertainment; and if she could not understand the Sunday services at Wrexham's picturesque church, she could comprehend her kind friend's translation and comments during the drive back to the farm.

On one of these occasions the spring cart, driven by Mrs. Parry's son, had to be drawn aside to make way for a passing carriage drawn by two small native ponies; and in which reclined a lady muffled up in furs, and accompanied by a portly gentleman.

In the former Muriel recognised Mrs. Wynne, and with a sudden exclamation clasped her hands elated; but the lady made no sign of recognition, and her companion was a stranger. The girl's countenance fell.

"Do you know that lady?" inquired Miss Williams.

"Yes, she is Mrs. Wynne, Captain Wynne's wife, mother of the young officer—you remember."

Yes; Miss Williams remembered; she had heard how Muriel chanced to know the young lieutenant; and she had an opinion that the lady might have distinguished Muriel in the cart, had she been so minded, but she only added, after a few words in Welsh with Mrs. Parry, "Mrs. Wynne is staying with the captain's relatives at the Plas, we may meet her again."

Meeting thus with Mrs. Wynne, sent Muriel's thoughts off at a tangent to the Forest, to wonder if the captain's servant was better, and if the robbers had been put in prison; and if they were the men Mrs. Kingsley fancied; and who that Maggy Blackburn was, for she had kept her ears open though her lips were closed. Then having landed at Waverham with Maggy Blackburn, the marvel of her Uncle Samuel's marriage filled her mind with speculations what her new aunt would be like, and when she would see her, and where they were going to live; and then home her thoughts flew to her mother, mourning for the loss of little George, and she had not a very bright face when the cart stopped at the farm-gate.

They did not meet with Mrs. Wynne again, although they wrapped themselves up and rambled over the mountains, making the most of the fine crisp weather, day after day. There is no question Muriel was disappointed, but she did not let disappointment mar her enjoyment. Indeed, she gathered a fund of more than health in those excursions. For to Rachel Williams—

> "Not a tree,
> A plant, a leaf, a blossom, but contained
> A folio volume. She could read, and read,
> And read again, and still find something new,—
> Something to please and something to instruct,—
> E'en in the noisome weed."

And though winter had stripped most of the leaves from the book of Nature, she could find—

> "Sermons in stone, books in the running brooks,
> And good in everything."

And so she fed Muriel's receptive mind with the purest thought, and led the girl to look herself for good in everything, even though the mountains wore no summer robes and the air was keen and cold.

It was well; for Muriel had gone to the Misses Briscoes' school under a delusion, only to experience a rough awakening. She went back *now*, re-invigorated and strengthened, to face evils of which she knew the worst, and determined, with the help of her Heavenly Father, to make the best of that which she could not remedy, and which might not be wholly evil.

It was well she went back to the chilly rooms, scant fare, wearisome exercises, and difficult tasks (not so much in books as needle-work) in so cheerful a spirit; it served to reconcile her somewhat to the severe discipline, and brighten the monotonous hardship of daily routine, not only for herself but for those with whom she came in contact: as Rachel Williams had brightened it for her.

Young Misses of the present generation have no conception what those hardships were at the period when the birch for personal castigation was considered an indispensable adjunct of even a fashionable seminary; when the set visits of music and dancing masters alone broke the monotony; and a letter or hamper from home put the whole school in a flutter, even though the contents were doled out, as it were, through a sieve.

It was quite an excitement when Miss Briscoe announced, with some stateliness, the arrival of "an eminent artist to paint Miss Ford's portrait" on white silk for the after embroidery of draperies and accessories in coloured silks by the favoured young lady; such portrait-taking being a sure indication of a coming removal from the establishment, and of friends willing to pay well for the distinction. Yet Muriel blurred a bright carnation in her own embroidery with a tear when she heard of the parting in store, for she had learned to love Alice Ford.

Two years,—two years more of study and privation,—and then Miss D'Anyer herself was invited "to have the honour of sitting to the celebrated artist;" but prior to that, her grandmother (who came duly for the great fairs, and brought just a few scraps of home news for the girl's hungry heart, and always a present for the Misses Briscoe) had carried off in triumph an embroidered posy with impossible stems adorned and tied with a sprawling blue bow, all on a circular disc of white satin, likewise a filigree basket and tea-caddy, a set of fine linen shirts, and a muslin apron of marvellously delicate workmanship, to be exhibited to the D'Anyers as a proof of Muriel's proficiency and her own wisdom in bearing her off to Miss Briscoe's renowned school.

She had no suspicion how many fines had been paid, how many tears shed by aching eyes over the "sixteen different openwork stitches" in the embroidered apron border which Miss Briscoe displayed with so much pride as "a credit to the school," or how often the rosebuds and forget-me-nots had bloomed and faded from the satin before completion. And so far had Muriel accepted the irremediable, that proud of her work and the commendations she received, she was too full of questions about those at home, during the brief visits of her Grandmother Bancroft or her father at fair-time, to think of complaining, had the opportunity been allowed.

Indeed, so rigidly was the dogma enforced, "Obey those in authority over you," that the complaint of a child or anyone *not* in authority, would have been disregarded, if indeed it did not suggest insubordination, and a more rigorous rule. And so long as Muriel was no worse off than the rest she would have felt ashamed to talk of hardship or accuse either Miss Briscoe or Miss Betty of inhumanity.

Consequently, when the Rev. Thomas Bancroft, mindful of his promise, called to ascertain how the young lady was progressing, he carried away only favourable impressions, setting down to youthful diffidence the hesitation of Muriel to answer, in the presence of Miss Briscoe, his questions, whether she was happy and comfortable. Muriel gained nothing by his brief visits, but the suave

Misses Briscoe did. The good report of the learned Head Master of the Grammar School was not to be despised, and they gained that by Muriel's uncomplaining silence.

Nay, she made no complaints during the midsummer holidays spent at Forest House, and if she looked thin, it was put down to over-growth and over-study.

She was too curious to ascertain what became of Captain Wynne's servant, and if the robbers had been caught, to say much about herself, though it did transpire that she had been punished because Arthur Wynne spoke to her, and that she had not been allowed to see the captain when he called.

"Ah, I daresay it was against the rules," said Mrs. Kingsley, polishing and dusting an oaken buffet or sideboard on which silver drinking vessels disputed precedence with china punchbowls. One of the former she took up and handed to Muriel, "See what the captain sent to my good man, and read what is on it, 'A token of a stranger's gratitude for genuine kindness and hearty hospitality.'

It's a fine cup; Kingsley's rare and proud of it, I can tell you. And look here, I'm just as proud of these." And she threw open a panel-door of the buffet to display a china tea-service over which a modern æsthete might rave.

"I suppose Mrs. Wynne sent you that," suggested Muriel, when she had sufficiently admired both.

"Not she! And if she had I should have sent it back. She gave herself too many fine airs to suit me. If the rest of the world wasn't born to wait on her she thought so. No, it came from the young man; the best of the lot; the only sociable one of the three. I daresay he had some of the family pride, but he didn't show it here. Kingsley and he got on famously together; and he looked well after that man Norris."

"I'm glad of that," said Muriel, "but you did not tell me——"

"Oh, I forgot. Aye, the thieves were caught as sure as they ever will be, but there were three or four folk, an ostler and a barmaid, and one or two others that swore an alibi, and so they got off, more's the pity! For, if there be two bigger rogues in all Cheshire than those Blackburns, I never saw an honest man. And that old mother of theirs is quite as bad. I wonder how Lydia and your Uncle——" Mrs. Kingsley stopped short suddenly, as if the vigorous rubbing of old oak demanded all her breath and her attention.

Muriel looked up—wondered—but she had asked what was an alibi, and Mrs. Kingsley launched into an explanation that it was a proof an accused person was somewhere else when a crime was committed; and then into compassion for Norris, who would be lame for the rest of his life, his hip having been "put out"; and Muriel went back to school without hearing what Mrs. Kingsley had to say about Uncle Sam and her new aunt; the aunt she had not seen.

Back to school, fresher and brighter; to grow pale and thin again as the months went on; and there was again a dreary winter holiday before her when all her schoolfellows were gone. But her good friend Miss Williams again came compassionately to the rescue, and Muriel was quite content to leave the good things in her Christmas-hamper for the Misses Briscoe, so long as she was carried off to spend another delightful vacation at Wrexham. The *last;* for soon after, to Muriel's great grief, she was called upon to part from her beloved teacher: that governess on whom the Misses Briscoe looked loftily down, yet to whom she, and not she alone, could point in all her after life as her exemplar; who had taught her that patient endurance might be sublime, and that *self* was a very small item in the sum of duty.

The naval officer had come ashore on leave and promotion. There was such a lovers' meeting in the spinsters' reception-room as ought to have brightened it up for ever. Then followed a happy wedding at St. John's, and a feast to all the boarders, over which the Misses Briscoe graciously presided in their best array, because they got all the credit and had none of the cost; then there was a general presentation of girlish tributes of esteem and affection.

And when at last the gallant Captain Griffiths carried off his bride in a post-chaise so many tears were shed for the loss of their gentle teacher, that Miss Briscoe nodded her head significantly and said in confidence to her sister, "It was time she went;" to which the echo responded, "So it was."

Thoughtful for others to the last, the newly-made wife contrived to make that a red-letter day for Muriel as well as herself, by the restoration of Deborah Massey's Bible, surrendered by Miss Briscoe at her urgent entreaty; and the few impressive words of farewell counsel which accompanied it were not likely to be soon forgotten.

Her departure was a loss to the whole school. Her successor was of another order. She strained discipline to hide her own incompetence, and made the girls' lives intolerable with fines and punishments, intensifying instead of softening the harsh rule of the principals. But if the good teacher was lost, her influence was not. In emulation of her example, it became Muriel's aim to screen or shield younger or more delicate girls from undeserved penalties, to lend her aid in difficult tasks, whether of book or work, and between her cares for others and the embroidery which was supposed to herald release, time passed less drearily.

She was now a tall, thin, dark-haired, brown-eyed maiden close upon fifteen, taking her place as monitress in due rotation; and, besides coming in for frequent short-commons in consequence, had many opportunities for self-denial. Then she had a child of eight in her charge in school and dormitory; and that which might have been a source of irritation to others, proved a very safety-valve for her pent-up affections. And surely never was one school-girl so cared for by another as was Polly Dutton.

Not only when lessons from Johnson's School Dictionary or Murray's Grammar had to be driven into a dull brain, but night after night in the severe depth of winter did Muriel sit up in bed, chafing the child's benumbed feet in the dark, to allay incipient chilblains when her own were in far worse plight. And who but she had the bravery to appeal to Miss Briscoe's humanity against the weekly promenade on the walls, and the double walk to morning service at St. John's and evening service at the Octagon Chapel on the Sunday, when the snow lay deep upon the ground, and every girl in the school had sore heels to be excoriated by the friction of shoes and pattens!

And what though Miss Briscoe stood aghast at her audacity, and lifting her mittened hands, declared :—

"It would bring ruin on the school! So long as Mr. Twemlow's young gentlemen can walk abroad for air and exercise, or to attend Divine service, our young ladies *must*. A single exception might be made; but as a *body—impossible!*"

What mattered it, so long as Muriel obtained immunity for the little one in her charge and two others, and induced Miss

Betty to prepare a whey of alum-and-milk to bathe affected feet! She was herself reprimanded; but she "had done *some* good," and was therewith content.

The snow lay on the ground for weeks. Miss Briscoe was inflexible. Through it the limping girls must plod so long as Mr. Twemlow's pupils went their wonted way. (They might, or might not, be in like condition.) Even Miss Betty ventured to expostulate (*she had* a slightly tender spot under the hard crust); but she was put down with, "Betty, I am surprised! We cannot afford to indulge in foolish sentiment. We must maintain appearances at any cost. The reputation of our school depends upon it. What would be thought if even half the girls were left at home? It would be ruin, utter ruin!"

As if she had invoked it, ruin came after the snow was gone, and of the general chilblains only the scars remained.

An epidemic broke out in the school, which was *not* to be concealed. Cestrian parents removed their children in alarm, and spread the rumour to others further afield. True to her creed, Miss Briscoe delayed communicating with friends until Doctor Wilmslow urged the necessity.

"But we shall lose all our pupils, sir," argued Miss Briscoe in dismay.

"Ye—es, madam, so I am a—afraid; but —a—I see no alternative. The healthy—a— a—must be removed—a—a—for their own safety." (The puffy little physician seemed to draw inspiration from the gold-headed cane which he tapped against his chin.) "Relatives will—a—I doubt not—a—appreciate your—a—thoughtful attention, and—a—a— self-sacrifice. And—a—I fear, madam—you would—a—be *certain* to lose them—a—otherwise."

"You do not think there is any real danger of the others, doctor, do you?" and the lace frill of her tall cap trembled as she spoke.

The doctor had a pecuniary interest in the Misses Briscoes' pupils; but he had also his professional reputation at stake.

"Well—um—a not if they—a—have a

careful — a — attention, such — a — as Miss D'Anyer gives to Miss — a — Dutton, and — a — you have space to separate the — a — cases."

"Separate! Why, sir, we have given up one dormitory to the invalids already! The house is like a hospital!"

"Without hospital conveniences!" thought the doctor, as he closed his lips with the gold knob of his cane, and bowed himself out.

And so thought Mrs. Bancroft when she came upon the scene about a week later.

Manchester had only just set about lighting, watching, and cleansing the town by Act of Parliament; it had not added a postman to its list of officials in the spring of 1793. The whole postal staff of the rich and thriving manufacturing centre, consisted of Miss Willett the post-mistress, and *two clerks!* Had not Sarah Bancroft, as a business woman, sent a trusty messenger to the small post-office in St. Ann's Square, twice or thrice a week, as did other merchants and traders, Miss Briscoe's tardy communication might have waited with its face to the window-pane until seen and demanded.

It was a dreary, drizzling February day. With a hood over her head to protect her cap, Mrs. Bancroft slipped her feet into pattens and crossed the wet yard to a long, low, timber, louvre-boarded shed, where her son stood to superintend the nailing of raw or damp skins fur downwards on dry boards, and the dusting or rubbing of powdered quicklime on others already stretched, such being at *that* time the cleansing and purifying process.

She had two open letters in her hand. "Eh! Sam, here's a pretty coil—read that," and she put Miss Briscoe's formal letter into his hand, whilst her quick eye went over the rows of skins set aside to dry, and those in preparation, and her equally quick tongue called out to a workman: "Lightly, lad, wi' th' lime, do'st mean to eat through the skin to th' fur! Thah lays it on th' chinchilli as thick as if 'twere bearskin."

"Well," said Sam, "and what's the coil? What if Muriel be ill, doesn't Miss Briscoe say there's no occasion for alarm, she will have every care and attention?"

"Ay, ay, lad! but read what Mrs. Hopley says, and then spell, and put together."

Mrs. Hopley was a mantua-maker in Watergate Street, Chester, patronized by the beautiful Lady Grosvenor, to whom she had been for many years own maid or housekeeper, until, late in life, she married the butler and speedily discovered that if she would have a garment to wear herself, she must begin to make garments for other people.

The buying of undressed skins (rabbits were classed and killed as vermin) had taken Mrs. Bancroft to Eaton Hall year by year, she had thus become acquainted with both, and now she supplied Mrs. Hopley with prepared furs for her aristocratic customers.

Mrs. Hopley's epistle would have been a mere order for court ermine for "my lady," with sable and mink in sets and for trimming for other customers, given with business-like precision, but for an afterthought, which found expression in a postcript.

"I think you have a grandchild at Miss Briscoe's. Of course you will send to remove her without delay; and if your messenger brought the furs, it would save carriage. What a direful calamity for Briscoe!"

It was a characteristic addendum.

"Well," said Sam, scratching his chin, "*that* means something. It's decidedly queer!"

"It means a journey to Chester for me, lad. I shall be off by the morning packet-boat, to catch the coach at Preston Brook; so get the furs sorted out and packed first thing. Whatever's the matter I'll see into it. And see you don't go to D'Anyer's, and frighten Ellen. And give that wife of yours a caution; though Lydia looks as if she could hold her tongue. I'll be back before the week's out."

"Ay, trust Lydia to keep a secret with any woman alive;" and a curious look came into Sam's half-shut eyes.

"I want no secret kept; I only recommend caution for Ellen's sake. Secrecy, sin, and sorrow begin wi' th' same letter; ay, and selfishness too. Keep clear of secrets, my lad!"

She had turned so abruptly that the peculiar expression of doubt and misgiving which suddenly settled on the face of that thirty-three years' "lad" was unseen. And if the clank of her pattens echoed any misgivings in Sarah Bancroft's own breast, they were not of her son Sam, or of her own unerring judgment, but of the Misses Briscoe, so bepraised in her grandchild's letters home. Mrs. Hopley's postcript pointed to something more than did Miss Briscoe's guarded epistle. She was "bound to see into it."

And she did, but was *not* back before the week was out.

CHAPTER IX.

A PROPOSAL.

WHEN ushered into the prim reception-room, so rich in specimens of needlework and caligraphy, and flattering testimonials, Mrs. Bancroft found herself in the midst of an excited group of strangers, to whom a surgeon named Prestbury, engaged by an anxious father, was enunciating his very decided opinion that the outbreak of disease in the school was mainly due to insufficient dietary, warmth, and water supply; and, in short, much that is now summed up as defective sanitation.

"Infamous! infamous!" ran round the room in a chorus. Guardians and relatives rose in a body from their high-backed embroidered chairs, and turned with one accord and all degrees of exasperation towards the two spinsters, who stood, with primly folded arms and compressed lips, to confront accusations and reproaches with dignified silence.

Denial was impossible, the condition of the suffering girls, the scant bedding, the crowded dormitories, needed little by way of evidence from young lips to confirm the surgeon's sorrowful testimony. Yet it was from young lips Mrs. Bancroft learned that Muriel had caught the infection whilst watching and tending Polly Dutton and others in the dormitory.

"She was *so* kind, and I am *so* sorry," said her little informant pitifully, adding, "And she read to us out of her beautiful Bible, and the 'Pilgrim's Progress,' and 'Evenings at Home,' and never seemed tired. No one reads to us now."

But Muriel made no complaint, she only said,—

"It was very well I was not taken ill at first, or Polly would have had no one to nurse her, and might not have got better so soon."

Getting better for any of them was not an

easy matter *there*, yet not an hotel in the town would open its doors to a patient from the infected school.

It was the break-up of the important establishment. By ones and twos the pupils were removed as speedily as safety permitted. Only the few who had escaped, and whose distant friends were uninformed, remained until the vacation, and of these not all returned.

It was in vain, by tardy attention to the sick, that the Misses Briscoe strove to rehabilitate themselves in public esteem and maintain their position. Strict discipline was allowable, but not starvation. The prestige of the school was gone; and after a struggle against fate, in a year or two they announced their "intention to retire."

Seeing no chance of her removal with the disorder at its height, energetic Mrs. Bancroft coolly took possession of Muriel's dormitory, as if it had been a hospital ward, and she the appointed nurse; a hint taken by two other pupils' feminine friends, whether to the chagrin or the satisfaction of the sisters there is no knowing. As for Mrs. Bancroft, she engaged her own doctor, sent in supplies, and took care that medicines and diet were duly administered.

She set aside Miss Briscoe and Miss Betty at the outset.

"Look you," said she, "don't you go near my grandchild with long faces and pitiful words as if you cared for her. All you care for is *money*. The little creatures committed to your charge have been no more to you than so many oranges, out of which you could squeeze the golden juice. And you've squeezed them a trifle too close at last. Here I am, and here I shall remain until there is a change one way or other. And if Mr. Prestbury's orders are not carried out, and aught happens to my dear child, if there's justice to be had in the Pentice Court, you shall suffer for it. I'll see to that."

And there, sure enough, did the hard-featured woman of business, whose soul was supposed to be wrapped up in her business, remain, watching night and day by Muriel's bed with unwavering affection; her bustling energy subdued to quiet, or expended on obstructives in the regions of the kitchen, to whom she soon laid down a law of her own.

Up and down stairs she went with the activity of a younger woman; indeed, if truth were told, sitting still to watch the thin face was like a penance to her.

At such times would her thoughts fly off to the furriery, wondering how Sam would manage without her; if orders were executed properly; if certain furs had been dressed satisfactorily; if wages and bills had been paid. Then her mind would revert to Ellen D'Anyer and her probable anxiety; and occasionally a still small voice would whisper that she had better have left the girl with her mother. But the whisper made her uneasy, and she resolutely closed her ears.

Then she blamed the Rev. Thomas Bancroft for keeping her in the dark; little thinking how he had been blinded on the one or two occasions he had made for seeing the girl, or how much the good man was occupied with his own concerns, his duties as clergyman, schoolmaster, author, and the father of a family.

She had trusted so much to his supervision when she brought Muriel to the Misses Briscoe; and now she blamed herself for trusting to anyone *but* herself.

There was only one thing she liked less than a silent watch; and that began when Muriel first showed signs of amendment, and expressed a desire that she would read her Bible *aloud* to her. She could not refuse; but surely never had Deborah Massey's Bible been opened less willingly.

Muriel's full eyes kindled at her favourite passages, unwitting that many a one was a searching probe to her grandmother's self-reliant soul.

Before Muriel left her bed the task required less effort, and by the time she was able to walk downstairs, Sarah Bancroft had resolved to renew her acquaintance with the large family Bible, mounted on the oak bureau at home.

Then followed a demand for Miss D'Anyer's

bill, and a business-like docking of exorbitant charges, never before disputed, ere Sarah Bancroft opened her canvas money-bag and laid her guineas down.

School-books and other belongings had already been gathered together, not forgetting the unfinished portrait, to be completed at home. An ostler came from the Plume of Feathers in Bridge Street for "the young lady's luggage." There was a tearful farewell to the remaining fragments of the broken-up school, poor motherless Polly Dutton sobbing on Muriel's neck. There was a more ceremonious and less affectionate leave-taking in the worsted-work apartment (where Mrs. Bancroft had spoken her mind pretty freely), an exchange of elaborate courtesies, and Muriel, who longed to say she was sorry for their misfortune, went down the outer steps for the last time; her freedom anticipated by fully three months.

She was not judged fit for a tedious journey; but her grandmother (who never lost sight of business, and so turned her involuntary presence in Chester to account), invited Mrs. Hopley's company, hired a boat at the Bridge Wharf, and the following day treated Muriel to a breezy row up the river to Eaton Park, the home of the Grosvenors. And it was a treat to Muriel, who had only seen the silvery Dee from the walls, and previously nothing wider than the fresh water Irwell and Irk, and had never put foot in a boat before.

As they walked, after landing, along the avenue of bare but stately trees, just swelling into bud, to the imposing and solid, if heavy, brick mansion Sir John Vanbrugh had designed (since superseded by a *palace*), and Muriel's brown eyes, ranging over the park (where indications that Spring was on the alert made themselves felt, and seen, and heard), were filled with silent delight, she was startled out of her dreamy rapture by the abrupt question of her grandmother,—

"Did'st ever hear or see anything more of that captain and his wife who had so narrow an escape in Delamere Forest?"

Muriel flushed with shame as she answered,

not shame for herself, but that which she had to tell of others.

"Well, grandmother, Mr. Arthur was on the Walls one day when the school went for the weekly airing; I scarcely knew him, for he had on a fine uniform, and looked so handsome, but he knew me, and came to shake hands with me, and then—and then, Miss Briscoes were angry, said he was 'rude' and 'impertinent,' threatened to write to somebody about him, and perhaps they did, for we never met him again—and I was reprimanded, and was sent to the dormitory."

"For what?" was the mutual interrogation of her companions.

"Why, it seems, I had broken the rules in speaking to him."

"Broken the fiddlesticks!" exclaimed Mrs. Bancroft indignantly. "I wish I'd known! Then I suppose that was the last of them."

"Well, I was told, as a great secret, by one of the monitors, that Captain Wynne called the next day, and asked for me, but Miss

Briscoe sent no message to me, and he never came again."

"Eh! And didn't the lady you had waited upon hand and foot come herself?"

"I don't know, I was never told. But I've *seen* her. I saw her the first time I was in Wrexham—the Christmas little Georgey died."

"Ah," interrupted her grandmother, "and when your Uncle Sam was married. Well?"

Muriel went on, "We were on a narrow road in Mrs. Parry's cart, and she met us in a carriage—but she didn't see me," and a sigh pointed the sentence.

"Wouldn't, more like. I've no notion of fine folk, who take your services as if they had a right to them, and are too proud to know you afterwards; but the lass has as good blood in her veins as they have, I know. Catch me putting myself out of the way for such people again! I hate ingratitude."

"Nay, grandmother," pleaded Muriel, "I don't think Mrs. Wynne ungrateful: you know she gave me that beautiful locket! and I'm certain Mr. Arthur was glad to see me."

"Well, well, child, have your own way!" was Mrs. Bancroft's conclusion of the argument. "The lass has more charity than I have," she whispered, aside to Mrs. Hopley; adding aloud, "But here we are, and now, Muriel, you can have a rest."

There was rest and a luncheon in the housekeeper's room, along with the housesteward and lady's maid, over which the elders chatted pleasantly; then Muriel, being still weak, was laid on a roomy sofa, whilst Mrs. Hopley had an interview with Lady Grosvenor, and Mrs. Bancroft with the head gamekeeper. Muriel was fatigued and drowsy; she was at length awaked from slumber by the housekeeper's invitation to show her the picture-gallery and other state apartments.

It was all new and wonderful to Muriel; and when at length they returned to Chester, she had forgotten all about the Wynnes and her grandmother's suggestion of ingratitude, which had given her some unpleasant sensations.

She was left the next morning to explore the city in which she had lived so long, and of which she had seen so little, whilst her grandmother made business calls on customers in the Rows.

The afternoon was given to a formal tea drinking at Mrs. Hopley's, where Muriel was treated with especial attention, not only as a convalescent, but as Mrs. Bancroft's grandchild.

Indeed, Mrs. Hopley—a little woman in a plain black stuff dress, of no fashion but her own—seemed to lay herself out to attract and entertain her younger guest; now a tall, thin girl of graceful bearing, and not uncomely face. Time had done wonders in the three years and a half she had spent in Chester, and if her flowing locks had been sacrificed in her recent illness, the old marks on her skin were rapidly disappearing.

There were hot wheat-cakes, and other Cheshire delicacies on the table, of which she was invited to partake freely. After tea she was taken to the show-room where Lady Grosvenor's court dress, suspended on an upright pole with cross-way pegs for arms, and inflated by a hoop, was displayed amongst others, most attractively.

"How do you like them, my dear?" questioned Mrs. Hopley graciously, after explaining to Muriel that hoops were worn at court, though out of fashion in private life; court-dress being appointed at the beginning of a reign, to be retained to the end; and the little plain woman in black gave a touch to a fold here, and a turn to drapery there, so as to catch the light and produce the best effect.

"Oh! very much;—at least, all but that purple velvet, I don't care for the way in which it is trimmed," answered truth-telling Muriel, whose instinctive taste was offended.

Mrs. Hopley lifted her eyebrows, "How would you have trimmed it?" she said with encouraging suavity.

"Oh, I'm not a mantua-maker," Muriel replied modestly, "but I *think* I should have liked it better this way," and she proceeded to a practical demonstration with some loose paper, and pins from her own pocket pincushion.

"My dear," cried Mrs. Hopley, "your admirable suggestion shall be carried out on another robe. I wish I had a young lady in my work-room with so much taste and discernment. Talent of that kind is instinctive." A few more questions were asked to draw Muriel out, and Mrs. Hopley,—who had made her acquaintance before, when growth had necessitated fresh garments,—exclaimed, "You might have been a milliner! What say you, Mrs. Bancroft, to leaving her with me as an apprentice. It's a thousand pities so much natural taste should be wasted; and if, as you tell me, there is a large family of girls, she would find a knowledge of dressmaking extremely useful—supposing she did not work for strangers," she added, observing the compression of the furrier's closed lips.

"She is going home with me to-morrow, Mrs. Hopley," was Sarah Bancroft's answer, somewhat doggedly given.

Mrs. Hopley returned to the charge. She

had seen Muriel's embroidery and tambour-work,* and had long desired to get one of Miss Briscoe's needlework pupils into her work-room, to replace one named Phœbe Horne who had been out of her time quite two years, and was missed.

"Yes, yes, of course; I don't mean now—but after a while" (she had said "leave her with me"). "You have known me long enough to trust her in my care; you know I have children of my own."

"Ay, ay, I know," was all the response.

Mrs. Hopley turned to Muriel, "Would you not like to be able to make and trim such robes as this," and she laid her finger lightly on a rich amber and black brocade.

"Oh, yes, if——"

Her "if" was cut short. "You hear, my friend?" and then after a pause—

"It is worth considering. Neither man nor woman should be without a trade, in these uncertain times. Riches take wing,

---

* So called from being worked on muslin or other material stretched on a frame as tightly as a drum. The tambour-needle resembles somewhat the modern crochet-hook.

and a living at the finger-ends does not. And *I* have not found mantua-making at all derogatory. *I* maintain a good position," and the little woman looked as if she knew her own importance.

"Well, well," said the furrier impatiently, "I'll see about it, I'll see about it," as if desirous to turn the conversation.

"That's right, *do!* I'll make the premium easy," persisted Mrs. Hopley as a clencher, "and we might shorten the seven years to five."

But no more was said, and the girl hoped no more would be said; she was not inclined to take kindly to the proposal, but she stood too much in awe of her grandmother to venture an opinion of her own unasked.

To untravelled Muriel, the homeward journey was something too exquisite for speech. The early March winds were keen, but Mrs. Bancroft declared, "I'd as lief be shut up in a hayloft or a snuff-box as be stifled inside a coach. Give me the breeze that blows the cobwebs off a body!" So they were outside passengers, their places having been taken and booked overnight; and as they were well wrapped up in warm woollen and fur, neither she nor the convalescent Muriel could take much harm.

She was not a talkative woman; and no sooner were the wheels in motion than her thoughts travelled with them to the warehouse and sheds left for more than three weeks to the sole care of Sam.

Muriel's joyous anticipations outstripped the horses; but the face of nature was newer to her; and in the freshness of its budding hopes was all in unison with her own, and from her high seat she gazed on the shifting panorama of meadow and upland, brook and river, farm and village, with feelings and emotions not to be put into words.

True, it was not the smiling month of sun and shower; but the trees had already sipped the wine of spring, and felt it throbbing in the furthest shoot. There was a ruddy flush of flowering bloom on the wych-elm and poplar, a tender green on meadow and hedgerow, where the lithe honeysuckle twined among the hawthorn's opening fans; and if only a solitary snowdrop lingered here and there, the crocus boldly lifted up its purple cup, the unostentatious daffodil by the wayside brook bent its head as it offered its incense to the passing breeze, and the coltsfoot had sent forth its golden stars to tell with perfumed breath that its broad leaves were coming by-and-bye. Now and again the love-song of the missel-thrush was half drowned in the rattle of the wheels; but Muriel felt as if she too must burst into song, so glad, so hopeful, and withal so thankful was she.

She was silent from excess of feeling; but even raptures do not last for hours, and coaches in the last century did not race with the wind.

A little child shivering by her side, to whom she extended the benefit of her cloak at Frodsham, helped to enliven the remainder of the journey with his prattle; but when they reached Preston Brook at eleven o'clock, she was almost too stiff and tired to alight. Her grandmother not more so.

The long, slow-going, ark-like packet-boat seemed indeed an ark of refuge after the shaking coach. The gliding motion was restful; she sat at the cabin window, listened to the ripple of the water, the occasional swish of the rope and the tread of feet overhead, watched the trees and houses on the canal bank slip past as in a dream, the glory of all being that she had left Miss Briscoe and Chester for ever, and was going back to the dear mother and sisters who must have missed her so much. The dream was broken in upon by a woman crushing past, who offered Eccles cakes and nettle beer for sale, by way of refreshment; but Mrs. Bancroft had a reticule basket well supplied, and there was tea to be had on board. There had need to be, for it was nearer seven than six o'clock when they reached the Castle wharf at Knot Mill (where Canute's castle is said to have been), and there was neither Sam nor conveyance to meet them.

They waited, the bustling passengers dispersed, yet no one came. Mrs. Bancroft's brows were knit, and her lips set over her strong teeth, telling of disquiet or displeasure, had there been light for Muriel to read the record. And still they waited.

"Do you think uncle received your letter?" asked Muriel at last, in some trepidation. "And what shall we do?"

"Eh! I don't know, child!" brusquely answered the first question, the characteristic "I'll see to it," the second.

There were as yet no hackney coaches, there was no place at hand whereat to hire a chaise. There were, however, sturdy men upon the wharf, one of whom Mrs. Bancroft found willing to act as porter, seeing there was no alternative but to take the man's honesty upon trust, and let him lead the way through dark, narrow Alport Street, and Deansgate, with Muriel's small hair-trunk on his shoulders, and Mrs. Bancroft's bag as a balance in the other hand, and to take the chance of meeting an empty sedan-chair by the way.

Neither Muriel nor Mrs. Bancroft cared to show all the alarm she felt; each had a dread of something wrong at home, to say nothing of the dangers of the streets or the two-mile walk at the end of a day's journey, but the man must have heard the tremour in Muriel's voice as she asked her grandmother if she thought the man could obtain one of the lanterns then flitting about the wharf among the shadows; for he put down the luggage with a civil, " Yoi, miss, aw thenk aw con ! " and in a few minutes a horn lantern was in Muriel's hand, the luggage once more shouldered, and they, thus lit, following closely on the man's heels with apprehension in their hearts.

Remember—for in this Chester was in advance of Manchester—there were as yet no public lamps, only private ones at a few of the better-class houses; that respectable women were not supposed to go abroad unattended after dusk; that there was no organized police, that drunkenness was a fashionable vice ; that footpads drove a brisk trade; and that the wild young men of the time thought it no shame to insult more peaceable people, even to the drawing of swords; and you will perhaps better understand the apprehension felt alike by the strongminded woman, who had a nice-looking young girl in her charge, and the inexperienced young girl herself.

CHAPTER X.

SAM'S FIRST.

NOT until they had gained the stand in St. Ann's Square, where paviors had begun their much-needed work, was an empty sedan to be found, and then so many more intrusive carousers had they met by the way than sober home-going townfolk, that Sarah Bancroft was glad to put her grandchild under the canopy of one, as much for security as conveyance. She scorned the extravagance of such a luxury for herself.

So the sturdy old dame trudged on by its ide, glad of the extra lantern swung on one of the forward poles of the sedan, as well as of the additional protection of the two stout chairmen. It was a late hour for reputable females to be abroad unattended.

It was close upon eight by St. Ann's Church

clock, when the prim rows of trees which sentinelled the aristocratic mansions in the Square were left behind, Mrs. Bancroft congratulating herself that the foul dark entry, with its "Dangerous Corner," so recently the only outlet from the Square to the Market Place, was done away with, and, losing sight of the narrowness of the New Exchange Street, thought only how soon the Exchange itself, with all its pillared façade, would be only a memory—and such a memory! Had she not seen the heads of the Jacobite leaders spiked atop? She supposed the queer old market cross and the pillory they were passing would be the next to go; things changed so fast since her young days. Her dreams of the past were put to flight by the activities of the present. The clock of the Collegiate or Old Church, towards which their faces were set, chimed the hour, and then the glorious bells rang out the curfew with a resonant dash.

In an off-street close to the shambles stood a dingy old public-house, known as the

"Punch House," and kept by John Shaw, at one time a dragoon, where throughout the day, and especially from four to eight in the evening, might be found the chief merchants and manufacturers discussing the news of the day and the prices of goods over their sixpenny or shilling jorums of punch, for which the military landlord had a special and occult receipt. But at the first stroke of eight did John Shaw enter his bar-parlour with " Eight o'clock, gentlemen; you must clear out." And out they went at the first bidding, for, did anyone presume to linger, the martinet's long-lashed whip cracked in their ears, or in came Molly, his factotum, with mop and pail, and flooded them out.

No one got drunk *there*. Some of the least steady-going and more exuberant spirits might, however, be primed for finishing the night elsewhere.

The chairmen were jogging along with their light burden under the shade of the overhanging black and white gable-fronted old buildings, not the less shadowy for the dim illumination of casements from within, when, simultaneously with the first clang of the bells, John Shaw drove forth the members of his club, six or eight of whom came on from the narrow bye-way, right in front of Mrs. Bancroft's party, one calling to another, "Who's for the Cockpit?" "Who's for the Bull's Head?" "Who's for the play?" "I'm off to the Blue Boar!" and so forth, blocking such pathway as there was. They were in the very height of jollity and merriment, some of them ripe for what they called fun.

"I say, old dame, with the lantern and basket, what treasure have you there you guard so carefully?" cried out one,—a tall, elegant man, in a fashionable suit of blue kerseymere, with shining buckles at his breeches' knees,—and he took a step forward as if to ascertain for himself. He stopped short, arrested by a stern, hard voice he knew well.

"Your daughter, John D'Anyer, who is fortunate in having a more faithful guardian than her father *this* night."

In an instant the long back bent, the Frenchified cylindrical hat was raised from the gentleman's powdered hair with a graceful flourish, not altogether due to John Shaw's punch.

"I—I beg pardon, Mrs. Bancroft; you have quite taken me by surprise. The imperfect light must excuse the discourtsey of my address. But how is it——"

She interrupted him. "Now, sir, don't make matters worse by excuses of that kind; nothing excuses rudeness to an old woman whoever she may——"

She broke off short. She had seen another figure warily edging off into the background as if to beat a retreat; the stealthiness of the action caused her to raise her lantern, and the light fell on the broad buckled shoes, the grey worsted stockings, the steel-buckled brown breeches, brown flap-pocketed waistcoat, wide deep-skirted coat, falling white neckcloth and disordered hair of her son Sam, with his three-cornered hat somewhat awry,—steady-going Sam!

"Stop, sir!" she cried imperatively, and he thought best to obey. "Where art thah sneaking off to? What hast thah done that thah cannot face me? Aye, thah may well be ashamed of leaving thy old mother and a young girl to come through the streets at night as they best could, and at the risk of insult. But I'll see into it. Move on, chairmen."

John D'Anyer was turning the handle of the sedan door, which Muriel could not open from within. She waved him back. "You can see Muriel to-morrow. You were in no such hurry to meet us on the quay."

John D'Anyer's pride was easily touched.

As she nodded to the men to proceed, and stepped forward herself, heedless of the jests and laughter of the dispersing party from the Punch House, leaving son and son-in-law to follow, or not, as might suit them best, he answered haughtily:

"As a *gentleman*, madam, if not as a father, I should have met you at the Quay had your coming been notified. As you did not think proper to acquaint *me* with your intended return, and so think proper to refuse me a word with my own daughter, I have no more to say. Good-night to both."

His hat was again raised, but with the sarcastic sweep of ultra ceremony, as if *he* bowed their dismissal.

Sam was a decided contrast to his brother-in-law, in more than the old-fashioned homeliness of his attire and manners. He professed to have less pride; he might have added that he had more policy.

They had neither of them taken sufficient punch to cloud their intellects, and, although somewhat elevated, the first shock of the unwelcome surprise had dispelled any vapours from its fumes. John's wounded pride led him to follow a couple of his companions into the open jaws of the Blue Boar, whose lair was a court off the other side the Market Place, where he talked loftily to his intimates of his character as a gentleman being at stake, and treated the said gentleman to so many soothing potations that he was anything but a gentleman when his rat-tat-tan on his door knocker roused the echoes of Broom Street at midnight.

Wiser Sam stuck close by his mother; excused his presence at John Shaw's, and his extra dose of punch, on the plea that a little daughter having arrived that day, he and John had "been merely wetting the child's head." And the excuse was sufficiently cogent, seeing that it was customary for a newly-made father to stand treat under his own roof, or in some bar-parlour to pay for the "glasses round," in which the health and long life of the new-born child were toasted and drunk.

She was barely satisfied, but she let it pass.

On like grounds he excused his unpardonable absence from Castle Quay. His extreme agitation and anxiety for Lydia had driven everything else out of his mind. He had forgotten to send to the Post Office that morning. Her letter of instruction would be lying there.

This was a much more heinous offence.

"A business man forget the post!" it sounded incredible! Hers might not be the only important missive lying neglected in Mrs. Willett's window! She was not so easily appeased. Yet Sam made his confession so naturally, and with so many genuine expressions of regret; he had such a firm hold of his mother's heart, and she such a firm belief in his integrity, that she softened at last, and said:—

"Well, Sam, lad, as it is thy first child, it may be excusable, and as thah's come and owned thy forgetfulness all straight up and above board, I may overlook it *this* time; but, prithee, be careful in the future. Punctuality and method are the hinges of trade, and a business man has no *business* to forget."

Sam's face was in deep shadow, so the uneasy expression which crossed it during the first portion of this speech was lost, and her sharply emphasized rebuke of his untradesmanlike forgetfulness might account for his temporary silence.

Presently, after a trade question or two, she began to ask about Lydia and the newly-born child, wished she had been a day earlier, and said;—

"I'd rather it had been a lad than a lass, for the first; but we must take what comes."

Again Sam's brows contracted uneasily and were not smoothed when she bethought herself to ask;

"Who's with Lydia?"

"Oh,—Maggy Blackburn," he answered, but not readily.

"Maggy Blackburn!" exclaimed his mother, in not too pleasant a tone. "Was there no one to be had nearer home?"

"Yea; but Lydia has known Maggy all her life, and I thought, as you were away, it was best to humour her, as she seems to have such a hankering after Waverham folk," he responded, as they stopped at his mother's house, and his hand went up to the door-knocker quite unnecessarily, seeing that the door opened with a mere turn of the handle.

Chairmen and porter were glad to exchange their loads for hard cash and foaming home-brewed ale, and, after spitting on the coins for luck, departed.

Muriel, notwithstanding the unsuspected tears shed when her father left her so readily, had fallen asleep by the way, owing as much to the motion of the vehicle as to her fatigue; and she was but half awake when she followed her grandmother into the large bright kitchen, where the stone floor was scrubbed as clean as the deal tables and dresser; and where Margery had put as bright a polish on the tall clock-case and oaken-settle as on the brass and copper utensils on walls and tall mantel-shelf.

On that same settle lay a boy about four years old, in clothes of a countrified cut, though they were good and respectable enough. He was a rosy-cheeked chubby fellow, and was fast asleep.

"Whose lad's this?" demanded Mrs. Bancroft, as sharply and briskly as if her journey and two mile walk were of no account.

"Eh? A nurse-choilt Maggy Blackburn browt wi her fro Waverham. Hoo* said hoo couldn't come bout† it. Measter browt it here to-day, to be out o' th' way," explained Margery, all in a fluster with the unexpected arrivals, and full of grief that there was "ne'er a foire anywheere but i' th' kitchen, and nowt but ham an' eggs for supper. Yo' moight ha' letten folks know."

"Never mind, Margery. If grandmother's as tired as I am, she won't care what she has for supper, or where she sits," said Muriel, dropping wearily to a seat on the settle beside the sleeping boy, on whom Mrs. Bancroft's keen glance was fixed.

"Sup, oh, anywhere," said the latter somewhat impatiently, as she left the kitchen to meet Sam in the passage. To him she put the same question she had put to Margery, to be answered again:

"A nurse-child of Maggy Blackburn's. She couldn't leave it with those rough sons of hers, so she brought him with her. She thought, as

---

* She. † Without.

he was but a little chap, we should not mind."

"Maggy Blackburn all out!" remarked the old lady, seemingly satisfied with his explanation, if not with Nurse Blackburn's easy assurance; and by the time their outer wraps were removed, and the savoury supper smoking on the board, her temporary irritation had vanished.

Still, her eyes strayed from her plate to the sleeping boy, as if there was something in his form or face which puzzled her; and Sam was not sorry when she proposed that the child should be carried to bed, saying it was "not fit to take the little fellow through the night air at that hour, whoever he belonged to."

"Whew!" he whistled to himself when well clear of his mother's door, "*that* storm's blown over! If ever I neglect to send for the letters again may I be hanged! And how she looked at the lad. I'd stand a guinea to know what she thought, that I would! Well I may tell Lydia the danger's over now, though it's been a close shave."

Thinking thus, and having escaped a dreadful catastrophe, it was with lightened feet and spirits he trod the uneven and winding way down Red Bank and Long Millgate, under the shadow of gable-fronted cottages (long since swept away), heedlessly stumbling over outlying steps, and at last coming into violent collision with one of the newly-appointed watchmen as he turned the sharp corner abruptly into Toad Lane, where he lived in one of his mother's houses; a row of which rose with the rising ground on the right-hand trending towards Hyde's Cross.

"Neaw then, tha drunken foo'! What dost mean?" blurted out angrily the custodian of the peace, steadying himself on the narrow path.

"Heigho!" cried Sam simultaneously and prophetically, "I think *this* might be called 'Dangerous Corner' with a vengeance!" and he gave himself a shake to restore his balance.

"A dangerous corner belike to thee, for I've hauve a moind to tak' thee t' th' watch-heause t' gie an acceawnt o' thisel';" and the lantern went up into the disconcerted face of Sam.

He had to put his hand in his pocket to find the heavily-coated man of lantern, rattle, and many capes, a heal-all, and that sent *him* home a little less elated, and the mollified watchman contentedly on his way, bawling, lustily, "Past ten o'clock, and a clear, dry night!"

Maggy Blackburn, a thin, lithe woman, with cold, light grey eyes, and what had been a ruddy face, dressed in a dark-blue linen bed-gown (or loose jacket) and linsey petticoat, with a white linen long-eared cap or mutch to keep her straggling grey locks in order, opened the door for him, and before he could say, "How's Lydia?" began to ask "Wheer's th' lad? Theer's no gettin' thoi wife to rest till she knows he's safe in th' heause."

At his answer, the woman, for many reasons a privileged individual in that household, uplifted both hands and voice: "Thy mother come back! an' seen th' lad! Eh! But I wouldna stand i' thy shoes, Sam Bancroft, fur summat! Thy mother has eyes to see through a brick wall."

It was an ancient black-and-white timber-and-rubble house, with short passages, queer turnings, odd stairs here and there, rooms of various sizes, shapes, and levels, intersected by beams, and lit by diamond-paned transomed windows. There was no lobby, or entrance-hall, the door opened into the common-household room, an oaken partition, or spear, about two yards high which projected far into the room from the doorway alone serving to screen the inmates from draughts, and maintain a show of privacy when strangers came to the door to make enquiries. Out of this room, almost in a line with the door, up two or three stairs, lay the short passage to the kitchen, to the dark and tortuous staircase, and to another room lit by diamond-paned, mullioned windows back and front. This, which had been comfortably furnished as a best parlour, and was kept in the most admirable order, went down a step or two; and it was into this room where a light was burning on a snap-table, Mr. Samuel had led the way, closing the door before he had committed himself to answer; when he did it was with a sort of wink:

"But what if dust be thrown in the eyes, Maggy?" and he slapped his thigh as if well pleased at his own dust-throwing; the wisdom of the punch-bowl in his self-satisfied half-shut optics.

"Some folks' eyes won't hold dust long. They may be blinded for a bit, but they see noan th' waur afterwards. I'd noan have left Jem behind. Folk as have secrets conna be too careful. But take thi shoon off an' come gradely up the stairs, an' tell Lydia it's a' reet. She'll happen believe yo. I don't."

And if Samuel Bancroft could have known how the face of that sleeping boy haunted the pillow of his mother, as a vague dream of something remembered through the mist of years, he would not have assured his anxious wife so glibly that it was "all right."

His confidence, however, served to set poor Lydia's aching heart at rest for the time, and when he kissed her and the babe and said "good-night," and went off to the spare bedroom, she closed her eyelids and went to sleep contentedly; with none of the misgivings that had troubled her mind for years, and which somehow seemed transferred to the brain of Sarah Bancroft.

Even with the many cares of her large business on her mind—business which she was no longer assured had been under vigilant supervision in her long absence, and which summoned her from sleep to work-rooms and ware-rooms at five in the morning, when the workmen entered the gate—she thought of him; nay, even in the midst of calculations during her hasty breakfast, she could pause to watch the boy eating his bowl of porridge by the side of Muriel, and ask his name.

"Jem," was the shy response.

"Jem what?"

"Maggy's Jem."

"And what besides?"

"Mammy's Jem."

"And who's your mammy?"

The boy looked with wondering eyes from Mrs. Bancroft to Muriel, but only replied, "Why, mammy's mammy."

He knew no more, and he could tell no more.

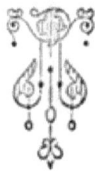

CHAPTER XI.

MURIEL'S RETURN HOME.

IT was well Muriel had been schooled in self-control, for the morning passed, noon came, dinner was despatched, and yet Mrs. Bancroft, who had sent for the delayed letters, could not spare time from her own pressing concerns to accompany the girl home, and she had forbidden her to go alone.

She took little Jem by the hand into the shed and warehouse to show how furs were dressed and prepared. The powdered lime, the smells, and the fluff soon drove them back. Then, keeping him still with her, she went for a stroll down Roger's Brow to see her cousin Milly—or Millicent—Hargreaves, whose father's dyeworks lay almost behind Mrs. Bancroft's place, but close to the river side, his house adjoining the works. They went through great gates, and a grassy croft set with rows of stout posts that bristled with spiky hooks, into a wet yard overlooked by the buildings which covered in the dye-pits, where men in coarse woollen overshirts, and thick clumsy leggings, with bare arms all red, or brown, or blue, went clattering about in clogs away from the carboys and dye stuffs, hanging up dripping hanks of yarn or pieces of cloth on the lines or tenter-hooks to dry, and the boy stared on all with wondering eyes.

When they had picked their way to the house, Muriel was sorry to hear that Milly was away, but Mrs. Hargreaves found them some cake and promised that Milly should soon come to see her in Broom Street; and as they went back through the yard they were met by the dyer himself, as rough-looking with his clogs and leggings and indigo-stained arms, as one of his own workpeople.

He shook hands heartily with Muriel, leaving his mark on her palm, asked a few questions, then, eyeing the boy askance, patted him on the head, saying:

"And what little chap's this? He favours thi Uncle Sam, I'll be hanged if he don't."

"He comes from Waverham. A woman they call Maggy Blackburn brought him with her. He says his name's Jem, and does not seem to know any other."

"Oh!" was all his acknowledgment of Muriel's answer; but when she went away, disappointed at not seeing Milly, he looked after them and gave a long whistle.

The banks of the Irk were not then all built upon. There were green spots here and there. She gathered a bunch of wild spring-flowers as they went back, for the chattering little one; then in the house again, sat down to sing ballads and hymns, and to play on the harpsichord, as much to still her impatience as to amuse the child.

She had a marvellously musical voice, and as its liquid notes floated through the rooms, Margery put down her work to listen; and, putting her head in at the open door, said:

"Eh! but aw fair thowt it wur an angel singin', aw did!"

"I don't feel very like an angel, Margery," she said with a laugh. "My feet are tingling with impatience to be off," and she rose to consult the tall kitchen clock, as she had done many times during the morning.

For not only was she most impatient to see those from whom she had been so long parted, but she feared to incur her father's displeasure and excite her dearly-loved mother's anxiety by lingering there, now that her return to Manchester was known.

Yet it was close upon three o'clock before Mrs. Bancroft looked into the front parlour, where Muriel sat with little Jem in the window-seat, showing the pictures in the big Family Bible (which apart from order-book and ledger constituted the family library), to keep him quiet, and said: "Be sharp and put your things on, and that lad's too. We may leave him at your Aunt Lydia's as we go."

Be sure no second bidding was needed. Up started Muriel, forgetting in her haste to put back the big Bible in its place on the bureau. It went no farther than the table, and there Sarah Bancroft found it at night. She was closing it with a mental reproof of Muriel's carelessness, when her eye was caught by a word or two of the large type. She sat down; the resolve made in Chester by her grandchild's bedside came freshly to mind. The great book which had lain so long on the bureau unopened, like so many a Family Bible, as a sort of dumb guarantor of the family Christianity, the silent custodian of its religion, lay with the seventh chapter of Matthew open before her, to strike, as it were, a shaft into her soul:

"Judge not, that ye be not judged."

Was it Muriel who had been careless or herself? Muriel had left the book *open*, she had more carelessly left it closed.

She sat down, and read, and pondered; that woman whose faith was in herself, whose soul was in her business, and as she read began to wonder if *she* was building her house on the rock, or on the sand?

Howsoever she answered the question to herself, she was more careful of the sacred volume in the future. During the week she was at business from early morning until late at night, but every Sunday afternoon, when she was alone, it came from its long resting-place to be read and studied.

Not too soon. There were disturbing influences at work, and the woman who had rested on herself so long, needed to find "the shadow of a great rock in a weary land."

But we are hastening too fast through that busy day. Muriel was well pleased to find her grandmother in a hurry: her own young feet had such a tendency to outstrip both the younger and the older ones.

Curious as Muriel had been to know what sort of a person was her Uncle Sam's wife, the introduction to the new aunt and cousin in the darkened room was soon over, and left her not much the wiser. The face she saw on the pillow had a sort of faded prettiness, though there was an ingrained colour on her cheeks, and the lips were close set when not speaking. And she was surely more than twenty-five, thought the niece, who had been told her age. But she had no desire to linger; even the pink baby had no charm to hold her that afternoon.

Indeed she thought her grandmother wasted time asking the queer nurse unnecessary questions about little Jem, and it was with quiet satisfaction that she gave him a kiss and wished him "good-bye," her face radiant with hope and expectation.

Yet the questions Sarah Bancroft had put to Maggy Blackburn had staggered the Waverham nurse, and her close set eyes contracted under catechism. She was, however, equal to any emergency, and her answers were satisfactorily true to the letter if not to the spirit. The catastrophe was averted—for the time.

With head erect, as befitted Miss Briscoe's pupil, Muriel tripped on lightly, glad that her grandmother only nodded to people she met in the crowded thoroughfare about Hyde's

Cross, instead of stopping to speak; but when at length the exclusive posts and chains of Broom Street were gained, and she saw her father standing without hat on their own doorstep, all Miss Briscoe's lessons in deportment were forgotten.

Children even in their teens were kept at formidable distances in those days, but human nature is stronger than custom. Muriel set off at a run to throw herself into his arms. Had she been alone he might have closed them round her in a fatherly embrace, for there is no doubt he had missed her. But the irritation of the previous night had not passed away with the fumes of John D'Anyer's potations. He had been called to order in the open street before both his own friends and common porters. He had been unwarrantably taxed with ungentlemanlike neglect, and anything more galling to the great foible of the fustian manufacturer was not possible. He had gone in from the warehouse to the noon-tide meal expecting to find his long absent daughter dutifully waiting to salute him with filial respect and affection. Her absence he had construed into a want of both, on her part, and as an intentional affront on that of Mrs. Bancroft. His amiable little wife had only made matters worse by suggesting excuses.

Several matters had gone wrong in the warehouse that afternoon—pieces of fustian had been spoiled in the cutting, and it did not improve matters when he came in the house at four o'clock for his tea, and saw no signs of Muriel. Instead of sitting down, he walked impatiently to the front door, and thus it was that the girl's open-armed advance received a check.

"I think, Miss, as you have been so long in finding your way *home*, you might almost as well go back where you came from."

"O father!" exclaimed Muriel in a tone of deep disappointment, as she clasped her open hands together in pain, and stopped short.

"She can do that, John D'Anyer, if she be not welcome here!" cried Mrs. Bancroft, coming up in time to hear him. "And if that's all the greeting thah has for the lass who pined for the sight of you all, till she could not eat her dinner, I think she's likely to go back sooner than thah counts for."

But Muriel had seen another figure in the hall, and flying past her father, who made way for her, was locked in the embrace of her dear mother, deaf and blind to all the world besides.

Sisters too, just home from school, bookbag and slate in hand, came rushing in the back way to surround and overwhelm her with kisses and questions, and drag her into the back sitting-room, where the tea-table was set, the toast and teapot being kept warm on a brass stool in front of the fire.

Meanwhile John D'Anyer, bowing stiffly to his wife's mother, ushered her ceremoniously into the front parlour before she spoke another word.

Much less ceremonious, she began first—

"See thi, John, I took that dear good lass away because I saw there was no proper place for her either on thy hearth or in thy heart. And if——"

She was interrupted.

"May I ask, madam, on what grounds you thus heap insult on indignity? You profess to have gauged my heart. I'm afraid you have not gauged my patience, which is not so long as to tolerate unfounded accusations even from Mrs. Bancroft, no later than last night."

It was her turn to interrupt.

"Stay, John; Sam was to blame for that. I had written desiring thee or him to be on the quay to meet the packet. It was not until we had parted in the Market Place that I discovered thah wert not in fault—that my letter was still at the Post Office—had not been sent for, in fact—and I am sorry I spoke so hastily. But I found what politeness an unknown old woman was likely to have met from thee and thi friends—and I found Samuel amongst the roysterers."

The listener bowed in acknowledgment of the apology, reddened as he found the tables turned upon him, but smiled covertly when Sam was mentioned.

"Ah, yes! wetting the child's head in John Shaw's punch!"

"Ay, and disturbing his own! Now, John D'Anyer," and she laid her mittened hand upon his coat sleeve, "thah'st a strong head and can stand carousing. Sam is not used to it. He would not have gone to the Punch House but for thee. Don't *thah* lead him into bad habits."

Astonishment, incredulity, scorn, sat on her interlocutor's handsome visage. He waved his hand loftily.

"Mr. Samuel Bancroft, madam, is not one to be led. Leading strings are not for men of *his* years and cool temperament. Mr. Samuel may certainly be trusted to take care of himself."

"So I thought till last night." And Mrs. Bancroft untied her bonnet strings, and sat down meditatively.

But he said no more, not even that he found his brother-in-law at the Punch House before him; such admission being contrary to his code of honour. And he scarcely came down from his stilts all the evening, though he did take Muriel in his arms at last, did extol her growth and upright carriage, and sent her to her sisters in a flush of delight. But he spoiled all by saying before she was fairly out of hearing, "What a fright that cropped head makes of the lass." He had last seen her with her hair rippling in waves below her waist.

"Be thankful you've got the lass back safe, crop or no crop," jerked out the old woman, who had been talking to her daughter about Lydia and just overheard him.

"Aye, mother," assented the younger one, as she poured out the tea, "we may be well content to let her hair go, so that we have her back safe and sound, seeing she has been so ill."

"Tchut! What has that to do with the lass being a fright? Would you have me thankful for *that*? Women have no sense!" Then having vented his explosive, John

D'Anyer turned the conversation, "Did you do any trade in Chester before you came back?" And Mrs. Bancroft, launching into her natural theme, lost her irritation.

This was not a very auspicious home-coming for Muriel. She could not forget her glimpse through the sedan window of her father and his companions, or the fright she had before he was recognized, and he, on his part, could not forget that she had so seen him. The want of cordiality in his first greeting was followed by a restraint not observed towards the others. He was conscious that his eldest daughter had seen him at a disadvantage, had seen him guilty of an act of discourtesy to an elderly stranger in the street, and wounded self-esteem suggested that her respect for him and his authority would thereby be lessened. In the clear eyes which said plainly enough, "Why am I not loved like the rest?" he read only the glance of a searching spirit to probe his soul, and not feeling comfortable himself, he was not likely to set her at ease. Added to that, the Reign of Terror in France, and the declaration of war with that country, affected English commerce, and he began to feel it. Annoyance on 'Change or in the warehouse meant irritability at home, and polite sarcasm on his own hearth, of which Ellen had hitherto had the chief benefit. Now, Muriel, throwing herself, as it were, as a soft cushion between them, came in for more than a share of his ill-humours and suspicions, nay, the very alacrity with which she ran to anticipate his wishes only increased his disfavour. "A pair of meek lackeys without a grain of spirit," he styled them on one occasion in his scornful cups; and yet the man could be generous and noble on occasion.

Nor were her sisters more amiable after the first few days. They felt themselves superseded, and began to be jealous of her superior manner and accomplishments, as one after another, aunts and cousins, came in and noticed her and her needle-work with outspoken admiration. Not so much the silken nosegay on the wall, in its circular gold frame, so prettily reflected in the circular convex mirror opposite between the velvet curtained windows, or the filigree-basket on the folded card table beneath the mirror, or the pair of tent-stitch footstools guarding the polished steel fender; as the embroidered portrait, which she sat in the light of one window to finish.

It was this, which being a novelty, eclipsed the nosegay; and was pronounced far beyond competition by the fingers of either cousin or sister. It was a tangible evidence of her superior endowments; since such work was only turned out of schools of high standing; and the minor matters of grammar, history, geography and arithmetic were thereby guaranteed.

Moreover, it was a well painted picture of a comely girl in a white dress, crimson shoes and sash, adorned with a gold-rimmed locket set with pearls, and with a glorious mass of brown hair flowing and rippling far below her waist. Overarching trees and a background of bushes threw out the graceful figure, which seemed in motion as did the fluttering canary on her finger, the ribbon which seemed to hold it safe, the floating ends of her sash, and the folds of her white robe.

The artist had quite been equal to his task, and the portraiture was faithful.

Marion and Anna envied the distinction. What right had she to have her portrait taken any more than they! And the feeling oozed out one day when Milly Hargreaves was present, admiring the picture, of which the hair, flesh, and sky were as the painter left them.

"It's well the painter put no marks on the skin to spoil its beauty," said Anna spitefully.

"Painters never do, even in large pictures," answered observant Milly. "Didn't the painter leave the wart off Cromwell's face?"

"Well, I'm sure Muriel's hair was never so long or beautiful as that!" asserted Marion, whose raven locks only rested on her shoulders.

"I dare say it was," struck in little Sara chivalrously, seeing the crimson rising in good-natured Muriel's cheeks; "Didn't you cry when they cut it all off?"

"No love, I was too ill." And Muriel sighed.

"Never mind, Muriel. It is sure to grow again," said Milly, reassuringly, as she noticed the moisture gathering in the mild brown eyes.

"I don't mind my hair, Milly—that is— (she corrected herself) I should not mind, but father does not like me without it;" and the moisture rounded to a tear.

"That's a very pretty locket," said Milly, still looking at the picture, with a kindly desire to change the subject; "Have you one like it?"

"Yes, the lady whose chaise broke down in Delamere Forest, gave it to me."

"Gave it to you? What for?"

"You may well ask what for?" jerked out Marion. "People are always giving *her* things. What did mother give her the old silver-clasped Bible for, I should like to know?"

"Ah, and grandmother gave her a fur-muff and tippet, but she didn't give us any!" added Anna, crossly.

"Perhaps she will when you are older;" suggested Milly; "but I should like to see the locket and hear all about it." And when she did hear all about it, Milly, who was half a year older and a bit of a sentimentalist, went into ecstasies about the romantic adventure, and the handsome young officer connected therewith, running into a whole chapter of possibilities and probabilities. At which Miss Marion again turned up her long nose.

From this it will be seen that kindliness did not spring up in Muriel's path at home.

Little Sara loved her, clung to her, slept in her arms at night, followed her about in the day, came to her hornbook in hand for help up the first and hardest steps to knowledge, or for a romp when work was over, but Marion and Anna took the cue from their father and in small indescribable ways strove "to bring the lady down a peg," especially Anna, who for some occult reason was his favourite.

At the same time they did not hesitate to take her gifts, or to tax her skill and obliging nature to the uttermost, and scarcely gave thanks for the willing service.

Besides Sara the only appreciative being in the household was her mother, and her smile was Muriel's ample reward. Was John D'Anyer's fastidious palate to be catered for, or baking, pickling, preserving, wine-making about, Muriel's untiring activity might be counted on; but whence came her patience and cheeriness under discouragement only her good mother knew.

She, however, had not been at home quite a fortnight, when her mother, whose stay-at-home habits were proverbial, taking advantage of her husband's absence on a business journey, and of a fine day, said she thought it was about time she went to see Lydia, and that if Muriel felt inclined she might bear her company.

The April sunshine was not brighter than the smile of Muriel as she tripped upstairs for her hat and cloak, and she carried something of the sunshine into the quaint old house and the shaded chamber where sat Lydia in a big easy-chair between the heavily draped four-post bed and the fire. She was wrapped in a blanket, had a pillow beneath her feet, and pillows behind her, all tokens of Maggy Blackburn's good nursing. Little Jem seated on a low stool by the fender had fallen fast asleep with his head resting against her knee. Her right hand lay caressingly on his head when they opened the door, but it was calmly folded in the other across her waist when they had made the circuit of the bed, and stood before her.

"How do you do, Aunt?" said Muriel in a low voice, accompanied by a graceful courtesy.

"How do you find yourself by this time, Lydia?" was Mrs. D'Anyer's first salutation, as she held her hand to the fire to take the chill off before offering it to her sister-in-law; "your nurse says you are both doing well."

"Aye, pretty well. But I thought you had forgotten me, Ellen," was the faint reply.

"Nay, I had not. Rheumatism came with the March winds, as usual, so I had to wait for fine weather and less pain, or you would have seen me sooner. So that's the little lad your nurse brought with her," Mrs. D'Anyer exclaimed, as the boy's brown head caught her attention. "I think she took a great liberty. Don't you?"

"Oh, no," answered Lydia, with the least possible tremour in her voice, which her hearers ascribed to weakness, "we knew she could not come without him."

"But what induced you to send so far for a nurse so encumbered? I could have recommended a very trustworthy person close at hand; Mother tells me she comes from Delamere, from the very heart of the forest."

Lydia shifted her head as if to change her position, and shade her face from the fire which had leapt into a blaze. "Well, her house is a goodish step from Waverham, but I've known Maggy all my life, and thought I should like her better than a stranger," was answered wearily.

At that moment in came the said Maggy, with cake and caudle on a tray for the visitors, checking Mrs. D'Anyer's next remark, "Mother says she has a very queer—" before the words "character from the Kingsley's," could be spoken. But whether Maggy overheard the speech or divined the thought, both Muriel and her mother were struck with the searching and anything but pleasant gleam of her light grey eyes, which seemed as though they would transfix the arrested speaker, whilst she bent her long back to wait upon them.

And Muriel thought the long ears of her linen mutch flapped as if shaken, whilst she interposed with the voice of one in authority, "Yo' munna talk so much, Lydia, till yo're stronger—and maybe ma'am, as yo' seem to be a mother yo'll bear me out. Oi've not ower much loikin' for early visitors mysel', they dun moore harm than good."

"Hush, Maggy," feebly remonstrated Mrs. Sam, "that lady is Mrs. D'Anyer, my sister-in-law; and I have not been talking much."

"Moore than yo' shouldn' oi've a notion," put in the woman with another strange look.

Mrs. D'Anyer rose, there was small inducement to prolong her visit. "Show us the infant, nurse," she said, with some little dignity, "and then we will retire."

The sleeping infant was lifted out of bed for inspection, duly kissed and admired, and then Muriel said: "I will come and nurse her for you, if mother will allow me, aunt. I used to nurse my poor brother George. How I wish *she* was a boy. Don't you, aunt?"

The aunt's reply was inaudible.

"You must not tease your aunt," said her mother, putting a gratuity in the hand of Maggy Blackburn, and then they departed. Neither observed that there were tears on the lashes of Lydia's closed eyes, or that her hand went back in a caress to the head of the still sleeping boy against her knee, as they turned away. Did she too wish that her firstborn had been a boy?

"We may as well walk on to Red Bank, now I am out, as your father will not be home until to-morrow, and after dinner you can run and see your cousin Milly, whilst I have a quiet hour with your grandmother." said Mrs. D'Anyer, turning down-hill towards Long Millgate, then a long, narrow and busy thoroughfare, between houses of all shapes and sizes, from the new red-brick mansion to the ricketty frame-built cottage of the working man; some up steps some down steps, with here and there a bay-windowed shop, where the light struggled through small panes set in thick frames. On the left, dark entries and narrow alleys ran steeply down the sand-stone bank to the very margin of the river Irk and shut it out of sight. Shut out of sight too if not of smell, the tanneries and dye-houses also on its margin, and the fair gardens and bleach-crofts across the stream.

Two or three streets broke the line on the townward side; and on both, more than one painted sign intimated that there might be had " good entertainment for man and beast."

On the lowest and outside step of one of these (the Queen Anne, whose painted effigy over the door was in good preservation) stood James Hargreaves, with his sleeves rolled up, his bare arms yellow with fustic, his leather breeches and leggings displaying samples of many dyes, just as rough-looking as when at his own works, more than a quarter of a mile away. He was, however, well known, and appearances were nothing to him, whatever they might be to his companion, a bleacher named Walker, whose croft lay across the unseen river, but whose attire showed no such intimacy with his vats and bucking keirs. Their two wives were closely related and they had business connections likewise to draw them together.

"Why, Ellen, is that thee! the sight's good for sore een! What's brought thee so far?" and out went the great yellow hand to grip hers heartily.

Before she could answer that she had "been to see how Lydia was getting on," the bleacher had also put forth a claim to notice; and James Hargreaves, chucking his niece under the chin with a couple of yellow fingers, said in a tone of pleasant banter: "So, Muriel, lass, you've begun betimes! Milly says you picked up a sweetheart in the wilds of Delamere: nothing less than a handsome young officer; and under the very nose of your grandmother!"

Muriel was abashed; her colour rose. She could only say, "Oh, uncle!" in a tone of remonstrance.

Her mother came to her aid. "Don't talk such nonsense to the girl, James. And your Milly ought to know better. Muriel was not twelve years old when she met those people in Delamere, and it is more than three years since she saw one of them."

As if reminded by association with Delamere, he remembered Lydia, and remembered something else. "I say, didn't thah see th' little lad from Waverham at Sam's?" he asked curiously.

"Yes, surely."

"What dost a' think of him?"

"He was asleep, with his head against Lydia's knee; I did not see his face."

"Then Lydia taks to th' lad? Oho! Well look at him when thah goes again, and tell us."

And with a nod, and a chuckle, and an injunction that they should "go and see th' old woman and Milly," he turned into the Queen Anne, after Mr. Walker, leaving both Mrs. D'Anyer and Muriel to wonder what there was remarkable to see in the boy.

There was the tinkle of a workyard bell, then of another, and another, a clatter of clogs on the stony pavement, of voices hailing one another, and the roads were alive with men and women, lads and lasses, and poor wee children hurrying home from dye works, bleach works, tanneries, factories, bearing all some tokens of their various callings in dress or person, the stains of some, the odour or the fluff of others.

"Poor little things," said Muriel, as two barefooted and ragged urchins of nine or ten years ran against her at the corner, "how hard it must be for them to get up at four in the morning and work in a buzzing factory all day, when the sun is shining in the sky and there are buttercups in the meadows. I never thought how much worse other children were off than myself, when I was at Miss Briscoe's."

"No, my dear, we are all naturally selfish, and in our own sorrows are apt to forget the greater ones of others; perhaps because we know and feel our own, and can only imagine those of others. But we must make haste or your grandmother will have sat down to dinner before we get there."

In another minute they were on Scotland Bridge; there was another stoppage. Samuel Bancroft hastening home to his dinner met them.

After ordinary greetings, Mrs. D'Anyer began:

"Sam, whose boy is that at your house? James Hargreaves has just asked me to look at him and say——"

Sam scowled. "Hang James Hargreaves!" he cried irritably. "Let him mind his own business. What's Maggy Blackburn's nurse-child to him, or to you either?" he added sharply, "that's Maggy's affair. *I* never asked her."

"Well, Sam, you need not get into a passion, I only repeated what——"

Again Sam interrupted:

"Yes, *only repeated*. That's the way mischief is made. I reckon you're going up to Red Bank to '*only repeat*' there. But I tell you what, Ellen, and you, Muriel, too, you'd best not say anything you see or hear about *my* house up *there*, or you'll find yourselves in the wrong box;" and with a monitory nod he stalked on.

He was not given to think aloud, or to mutter as he went, but with his lips close set, his thoughts kept pace with his steps, and thus they ran:

"Hang it all! This comes of giving way to Lydia. A pretty coil there'll be if mother gets hold of the clue. It was sure some imp of mischief kept me from the Post Office that day, and sent the poor little lad right in mother's way. It's confoundedly awkward! confoundedly!" And whilst he meditated he scratched his chin, and looked vacantly at the ground as he went. Presently a cunning gleam shot into his eyes; he had found a cause for self-gratulation. "It was lucky I met Ellen and Muriel. I've got to know what's in the wind, and that's something. And I think I've frightened both of them into silence. Neither one or the other has the courage of a mouse, and I'd lay odds they say nothing to mother that's likely to come back to me."

He was right so far, that nothing *was* said, but whether from lack of courage, or from lack of interest in the subject, or the pressure of more interesting topics, is another matter.

Ellen D'Anyer had certainly remarked to Muriel:

"Your Uncle Sam seems put out about that boy. And no wonder. He's not overfond of children, and I daresay he is savage at the nurse bringing another person's child into his house to be kept. Perhaps your grandmother has been grumbling about it. I know she said it was like Maggy Blackburn's impudence to bring it. So we had best say nothing about it, we may only make mischief. Lydia seems half afraid of the woman; and it's not safe to offend her, seeing how often your father has to cross the forest and the rough character of her two sons. You know they narrowly escaped the gallows over the attack on that captain's servant."

"Yes, Mrs. Kingsley told me. She said there had been some false swearing or they would never have got off. Perhaps Aunt Lydia only had her for a nurse, on account of Uncle Sam's travelling."

However this might be, Uncle Sam's courage led him to disturb his sick wife's serenity that day by grumbling at the presence of both Maggy and little Jem, and to eat his dinner with no worse relish for leaving her in tears.

And when Muriel went a few days later to inquire after her Aunt Lydia, she found her downstairs, weak and low spirited, with a fretful child, and no nurse or attendant but a rough servant-lass not more than fourteen.

Sam had "bundled Maggy and the boy both off," with little apparent regard either for his wife's condition or her tears.

Lydia did not say this, she merely explained that "Maggy Blackburn was obliged to go back to Cheshire; and I am very sorry, for I cannot keep baby quiet."

"Let me try," said Muriel, and walking about the room with the velvet face nestled to her own she lulled it to sleep after a time. Then seeing that Lydia was making feeble attempts to "put the disordered room to rights," she bade her sit down and she would do it.

When Sam came in for his tea he saw

Muriel installed in the place of Maggy Blackburn, with her mother's approval, she having hurried home to obtain it.

"I found Aunt Lydia all alone, with the baby crying on her lap, and her eyes were red as if she was fretting over her own inability to manage it," she had said, nothing doubting her own accuracy.

Fretting, from whatever cause, is not conducive to a patient's recovery, and quite three more weeks elapsed before Lydia was strong enough to take charge of her own household affairs.

"You're born for a nurse, Muriel, in spite of your grandmother," Sam had said before she had been there many days; Lydia had seemed to appreciate the gentleness of her tone, manner, and movements, and the unwonted daintiness with which her meals were served; and both were hearty and sincere in their thanks when she left; but for all that she had a lurking suspicion that they would feel her absence a relief.

"There's no place like home, mother dear,"

said she, as she untied her bonnet-strings in their own snug sitting-room; "I did not feel much like *home* at Uncle Sam's; and I don't think Aunt Lydia feels so either, she sighed so heavily if I chanced to mention Delamere or the Kingsleys, or the Wynnes; I could see she checked herself in speaking and shut her mouth tight. She never seems free and open, but always under some restraint, especially when Uncle Sam is there; and I am afraid she is unhappy."

"May be so, my dear, long courtships and late marriages do not always ensure felicity, whatever your grandmother may think."

Nor did early and hasty ones, if her own might be taken as a sample. Not that John D'Anyer did not estimate his wife in his best moods. But he set so much larger an estimate on himself, was so thoroughly imbued with personal vanity, and his claim to gentility —though his own father was only a manufacturer—had such extravagant ideas of his supreme right as lord and master to worship and obedience, and was so easily flattered out of doors into excesses which sent him home in his worst moods, that the poor little wife might have been excused had she joined her mother in deprecating early marriages.

END OF VOL. I.

www.ingramcontent.com/pod-product-compliance
Lightning Source LLC
Chambersburg PA
CBHW031741230426
43669CB00007B/431